"Oregon is more than mountains and sea; it is my history, my attitude, my compass."

All works created by author
For more information visit www.michaelbkofford.com

Trail to Tale

by

Michael Kofford

MBK Publishing

Dedication

For my parents who were so tolerant of me growing up,

my wife for her patience with my writing bug,

Kris for sticking with an oddball,

and Dee for her wonderful

editing and friendship.

Table of Contents

Introduction

Oregon has always been my home. I've left the nest to live in other states for school or jobs, but something about that angry deep green water on the coast and the ever-present threat of South Sister (volcano) turning active always seemed to bring me back like a homing pigeon. Oregon has become an addiction for visitors these days as they constantly cruise by my mother's place near Cannon Beach searching for that last plot overlooked by the big realty offices. Further east, the city of Bend had swollen to the staggering population of 94,000 by 2019. This former gas stop and home to a community college, now boasts 23 brew pubs and a 5 p.m. traffic jam filled with Mercedes and BMW's. Portlanders meanwhile, will tell you there is no gray area about feelings for their city. You either love it for its creative, deeply committed passion, or despise it for its oddball liberal tenacity. I always admired the city myself, but during a discussion with farmers thirty miles south, learned how much they professed to "hate" the city, avoiding it for everything but the airport. As with the nation, Oregon is bitterly divided, making me wonder how different Oregon must have been in its simplicity a mere 155 years before, beckoning farmers at the end of the American Civil War.

When you cross into Oregon from Idaho off Highway 84, just below the small town of Ontario, you are greeted by the green banks of the Snake River located on the north end of the Owyhee Uplands. Whenever I reach this area with its low-slung forested hills and long stretched valleys, I think of that promise it held for my ancestors making the long trek from Independence, Missouri along the Oregon Trail. The opportunity to sink a plow into rich earth after a long journey through dry, grassy plains and the difficult Rocky Mountains, must have been tempting beyond words. So tempting in fact, my relatives didn't make it to Oregon City, instead stopping in the small vale of Cove outside La Grande in the Blue Mountains region. As you descend to Baker City north of Ontario, you see the Blue Mountains approaching, topped with snow. You find yourself driving through rocky canyons one moment, then richly diverse forested mountain sides the next. My father worked at a lumber mill up here when he was in high school. He was tall and lanky, and everyone waited for the inevitable splash into the mill pond that never came.

Take the opposite way south from your Idaho entry point, and you'll follow the uplands down to the largest block fault mountain in North America: The Steens. If you drive into the area from the west, you follow a long upward slope into juniper forests crested by stone. I saw my first pair of Horned Larks at the peak of this range, and once had the friendly visitor center ranger show up at my campsite just before midnight. He wanted to exchange stories, but the experience flustered my wife a bit, who wasn't used to late night callers while residing in a tent. If you drive along the eastern boundary of the thrust fault, you'll see the massive uplift snapped like a cracker from years of pulling and stretching in tectonic battle. I don't doubt I'd be a geologist to this day if I'd seen that wondrous cliff side rising from the high desert floor as a six-year-old.

Continuing south you'll find what has been called Oregon's Outback, where after reaching the tiny town of Fields (great stop for burgers), you head west into Basin country. Be sure to wave back to every passing farm worker, as they mean it. But that doesn't keep it from being some of the meanest John Wayne dry, dusty, scrubby real estate in the West. I used to choose vacation themes for my summers when I was teaching and this area came up during my hot springs year. I visited an isolated watering hole just south of Hart Mountain. Some of the lonely characters finding their way out in that burning summer hell spoke to the character of the place. One old timer, red and naked in the dull green water sparkling with light, told the tale of the governor who once strolled out to this very spot in the seventies for a mid-day soak. As he spoke, groups of prong horned antelope danced in the sagebrush searching for mates. If I recall correctly, they are the fastest hoofed mammal in the world, even without any real predators (beside man). If you're a birder, Malhuer Lake is a must, as you'll see how even a colorful Northern Oriel seems to fit in with the landscape, among the bobbing Brown Pelicans, like the last piece of a jigsaw puzzle.

Back in La Grande, an exit from the highway takes you through the downtown where things have barely been altered since the time my parents attended high school here in the fifties. The quaint little malt shop, the drive through burger place, and even the barn my great uncles raised after returning from WW2, are still there. The difference comes through the people. Skinny ties, tortoise shell glasses, and overalls have disappeared, traded for a generation preferring lattes, sleeveless shirts, and sweatpants. Isolation, it seems, has not protected locals from texting and social media culture; but still, the land will continue on as the eternal backdrop for my family history. I was fortunate enough to spend one summer in the Blue Mountains working on an archaeological survey south of Heppner. An old German professor led a patchwork of scruffy, torn jean rejects, who walked the backcountry looking for cultural artifacts. I was also able to experience the grave reality of cattle "blowouts" caused by their grinding hooves. Along with devastation from boring beetles, it was disheartening to see how virgin forest could be so quickly damaged.

Mount Washington

Continuing north, the highway rounds the corner of NE Oregon at Pendleton, and continues into the Columbia Plateau to Portland. Famous for its "Round-Up" Rodeo and blankets, sunbaked Pendleton gives little indication of the beauty that awaits travelers as they pass the Umatilla Bridge toward Boardman. Crossing into a broad, ancient basaltic lava bed, one can only imagine a time when shield volcanoes ruled the day here. Upon gaining the company of the Columbia River, a short, but tedious drive ends among blackened columnar basalts with rounded high cliffs on the Washington side. Covered by dry, tan grasses in summer, these features were referred to as the "butt mountains" by my sister during family trips. On the Oregon side, cast shadows

play among islands of basalt creating new shapes and playgrounds for the mind. I frequently found myself lost in the muse of mythic dreaming while passing late in the day before a creeping, bright sun. The Columbia Gorge is one of the true joys of my life as one finds sailboarders near The Dalles before enjoying Hood River's apples, cherries, and brew pubs before the final push to Portland.

At some point along this journey, the twisting road following the relentless Columbia makes a hard downward left, affording a breathtaking view of the King of the Cascades, Mount Hood. Topped in snow, the majestic 11,250-foot mountain may not be the highest in the chain, but certainly is a memorable stunner before the Gorge narrows into a lip of greenery, passing thin wispy falls and isolated towns. I've struggled a few times trying to keep a steady hand driving as the view of Mount Hood became too inviting for at least a single photo. Timberline Lodge, sitting 6,000 feet up the south side of the mountain, was built by the WPA in 1937, and has marvelous skiing and fairytale hikes if you don't mind its increasing popularity. As you near the end of the Gorge, no visit is complete without a stop at Multnomah Falls. The silvery two stepped beefy falls must have been a sight for sore eyes during the Lewis and Clark expedition and has changed little since their epic canoe drive-by over 200 years ago. During my last trip, I heard so many different languages near the gift shop, I actually started inquiring as to the point of origin for many of the people talking there.

As Portland finally comes into view, the Columbia turns north as Highway 205 heads south, melting into I-5 and entering the most populous section of Oregon: The Willamette Valley. This green corridor of rich farmland is framed by miles of vineyards, hazelnut groves, and pockets of sheep. The south end is anchored by Eugene and the University of Oregon where I attended during the 1980's. I saw Bob Dylan and the Grateful Dead in Autzen Stadium, attended a writer's workshop with Ken Kesey, shook hands with Timothy Leary, and attended a Hunter S. Thompson lecture at McArthur Court. The city housed a mix of refugees from the sixties, many brewing their own beer in basements, and wearing strange costumes at social gatherings. Hippies, I recall, were the first to master the art of the fresh fruit smoothy. A truly unique place for coming of age after a turbulent time.

South of Eugene, passing south through Roseburg, the SW corner of Oregon is dominated by the Klamath Mountains region. The area contains beautiful rivers such as the Rogue, favored by Clark Gable for fishing, and The Rogue River Creamery in Medford, home of the world champion cheese for 2019, The Rogue River Blue. A favorite drive of mine in the Fall is near the California border. Here, trees are often covered in fog as forest and farms intermingle before entering the quaint little city of Ashland.

The famed gigantic redwoods of Northern California extend into Oregon with a diversity of coniferous species including Douglas Fir, Mountain Hemlock, Port Orford Cedar, Ponderosa Pine, White Fir, Brewer Spruce, Red Fir, Western Red Cedar and Pacific Yew, as well as other curious trees such as the massive-coned Sugar Pine.

A turn north from Crescent City on Highway 101 is perhaps one of my favorite stretches of coastline in the world. I once walked through an early morning fog onto a beach near Brookings to find I was sharing the space with a sizable herd of white tail deer. It's lovely to see deer prints crossing soft beach sand. Roosevelt elk are another familiar site along most of the coastline. There are novelties such as the Prehistoric Garden near Ophir, and dynamic old school bridges in Coos Bay, Newport, and Astoria. When I was a child, Lincoln City was known for two things: saltwater taffy, and the marvelously weird Pixie Kitchen; my first introduction to video games, hush puppies, and wheat thins. Blown glass has become the latest attraction along with wine tasting rooms, as an ever-evolving mix of new fusion restaurants takes hold. For me, the highlight of Oregon will always be the public beaches, the amazing nature preserves, and those wonderful rocky outcrops forever being hammered by the angry waves of the Pacific.

No tour of Oregon would be complete, without a look at those choosing to live here. A hundred and sixty years after my relatives stepped out of their covered wagons, the state has shifted into the red/blue zones we've seen nationally, where rural farmers with a taste for conspiracy theories and guns grumble, while young urban rich techies live on lattes and haunt jolly brew pubs. The Oregon I grew up in was much simpler. Every boy played baseball, every girl had an easy bake oven and we all shed a tear during the National Anthem.

Famed cultural icon, Charles Kuralt, once described our citizens in a short film this way: we were a state with a diverse set of views honored and respected as a way to maintain our social cohesion. This lines up nicely with my perceptions as a youth growing up in the state; we saw each other, talked things out, and weren't so concerned about just being right. Certainly, there was pressure for social conformity as rural communities entered the seventies feeling the sting of the sixties on their values. Upper classmen at my Junior High invented "treeing" as a common way to reprimand young upstarts for getting out of line in the halls. This was accomplished by grabbing each of the ankles of a young man firmly, before pulling them on opposite sides of a young sapling to exert great pressure upon the testicles. I got the message and towed the line, choosing not cause trouble. This provides insight into Nixon's landslide in my county during the 1960 election where 70% of ballots landed red. We were a conservative state that eventually outgrew its roots in order to face and adapt to modern challenges such as violent clashes with police after the George Floyd killing. Trial by fire testing the limits of new age liberalism through smashed glass and chaos in the streets.

Perhaps one modern threshold remains in the evolution of our blue-ness. While the "Keep Portland Weird" culture has succeeded in holding art, coffee, and community as primary, there remains a meddlesome thorn in the side of a city pumping out high end apartments like car parts. A friend who moved from Texas five years ago mentioned how much she missed the waiters in Portland during a visit back home.

"Portland waiters don't just serve you your food," she said, "they interact with you and ask questions about how your day was before writing down precise instructions on how to cook your burger. When I went home, it was like Texas waiters were barely competent, hardly able to talk and write at the same time."

With such bliss, how could there be hypocrisy? With new arrivals, the city has inherited a fleet of Mercedes and BMWs to flex its muscles into the modern era. Today's covered wagon, high tech vehicles often parked mere feet from the tent cities and broken-down RVs of the wandering homeless. I once pulled over to get my bearings in east Portland, where I noticed a line of tents extending along the city side of the sidewalk. Nearby, a homeless woman lay passed out on the pavement, face down. Being concerned, I

squinted to see if I could tell if the woman was breathing when someone emerged from the nearby upscale apartments in a trot. Thank God, I thought, someone is coming to make sure she's ok. This thirty-something professional promptly stepped over the body so he could quickly move his Mercedes out of the sun and into the shade of a nearby tree. I asked myself, is our humanity only in play when it pays an entrance fee at the door? I pondered the cultural change.

Certainly, our state faces some daunting challenges, but when I think back on the people who came before, those sturdy old survivors of The Great Depression and World War 2, I have faith we will one day compromise and move forward together. There is equal love for our hard-working skeptical farmers, as I possess for our pretentious, beret-wearing artists. This state has always been comprised of outcasts in one shape or another, but they have always been hammered into Oregonians who don't tan, they rust. This book is a love letter to my beloved Oregon. Your lack of perfection, your goofballs and professionals, your angry zine authors, your over intellectualized wine tastings, and your truly phenomenal landscapes, are home. A home I have moved away from many times, but always wander back to with a warm feeling in my heart and smile upon my face.

Prologue

When I began organizing my thoughts about the ways my home state had influenced my life, I considered the journey of the old brass bed occupying my upstairs guest room. Scratched, dented, and presently gathering dust, the once luxury item held a place of honor in the home of a distant relative. Valuable enough, in fact, to be included in the scant possessions stuffed in a wagon after the destructive American Civil War and carried across the Rocky Mountains on the renowned Oregon Trail.

The piece would exchange hands many times over the years before being pulled from a dark corner in grandmother's attic and given to my sister, and then later, landing with me. It filled my barely-adequate bedroom through high school until finding its way, once again, into a relative's garage during college. There it sat for five years until my living conditions settled enough, and I returned to fetch it once again. Some things in our lives should never be scrapped. They run so deeply through our

"Life should not be a journey to the grave with the intention of arriving safely in a pretty and well-preserved body, but rather to skid in broadside in a cloud of smoke, thoroughly used up, totally worn out, and loudly proclaiming "Wow! What a Ride!"

— Hunter S. Thompson

past, our sense of place, and who we are as individuals, we continue to carry them along until they are a part of us, our unique fingerprint upon history. Somewhere in that history, I became a part of Oregon.

Just like her coastal salmon, I pitch myself against the rocks and swim upstream, eventually returning home after each lengthy absence, my childhood memories refreshed new with visits to treasured spots and isolated locations. There is something in the sense of place that is baked into us, ingredients drawn from the common experience of youth that challenge and brand us with the unique identity of Westerner.

Who are we if we cannot claim a place as home beyond the gathering of a few possessions? We are lost at sea without mountains to cling to, destined to wander featureless prairies until exhausted by the struggle. To my great uncles, my grandparents, and friends, thank you for the wisdom you taught, the patience you showed, and the brass bed you gifted me. I will treasure you all to my last inevitable breath, whereupon my ashes shall join the land I love.

The Richards side of the family in the 19th century

Chapter 1

Farm Life

"I had rather be on my farm than
be emperor of the world."

-George Washington

My genes were sown in farm country, though I am of the first generation in a long line of family that didn't grow up tending fields or riding to school on horseback. When my parents married, like many rural kids, they wanted a new life for their children, a piece of the American Dream that could only be found in the city. They decided to leave the quiet solitude of farm life for dad's teaching job in the then small town of McMinnville, a mere thirty-five miles from the soon to be bursting city of Portland. They purchased a ranch style home built in 1963 of old growth redwood for a then whopping $16,000. As kids, Portland was a boon as we always seemed to have a shot at the newest bicycle or fad for our birthdays. Plus, there were experiences only the suburbs could offer: shopping, art shows, concerts, street bustle, and even exotic restaurants like Taco Bell. Somehow, through it all, we managed to stay farm folk at our core; always drawn back to the land, learning to tie our own flies, hike the Pacific Crest Trail, and photograph mountains with our boxy black and white cameras.

Mom and Dad's Wedding

I learned to ride horseback on my Great Uncle's farm during grade school, but the time was too short to encompass the full farm experience. Fate would intervene with a major life change in 2017, bringing my family past to life once more, front and center. I lived out of state for a decade, worn out by a string of forgettable jobs, looking for some escape when my wife was offered her previous

Mount Hood

Vineyard on the farm.

"Farming looks mighty easy when your plow is a pencil, and you're a thousand miles from the corn field."

-President Dwight D. Eisenhower

teaching position from ten years earlier. We sold our house, packed up our things, and headed back to farm country. My best friend still lived on the edge of town, taking advantage of a construction boom as McMinnville erupted in a wine explosion, luring much of the world to our small city with its vineyards and tasting rooms. Our quaint timber and farming town suddenly became a hip cultural center featured in magazines and newspapers. Even a large billboard, just up the road on the outskirts of Newberg, announced the "Land of Plenty" awaiting those willing to venture a little further. All the changes made the move seem different and new, but the boom had left housing prices in the clouds, so we posted a general request on social media, asking old friends about affordable rentals.

As luck would have it, a former colleague of my wife's had just such a place. Her family had decided to rent their original 1895 homestead seven miles outside town, seeking someone who could respect the old box western without the police visits and drug deals of the former renters. It sat on 350 acres of partially forested land with delicious purple Italian plums, cherries, three vineyards, and an old growth pear tree just uphill from the back lawn. A short walk led to a spring that supplied both drinking water and life blood for crops, creating two small ponds along the route of an overgrown stream. At last, I'd get my chance to return to the lifestyle of my ancestors and experience the country life they made for themselves at the end of the Oregon Trail after the Civil War.

I knew farms required a lot of hard work as the first job for most kids in my town involved catching a beat-up-old-school bus to go pick berries or beans every June. The goal was earning enough money for school clothes, so we thought, but actually introduced us to the country work ethic necessary for rural survival. I still have great memories of the row boss punching holes with her clicker in the green count card for each new crate, and the frozen Shasta colas wrapped in foil by mom the night before so our drinks would remain cold. Some of the strawberry row wars will live in my mind forever. Once you happened upon a rotten berry, you'd keep an

OREGON 5

eye out for the row boss, then fire off a volley in one sweeping motion at the nearest competitor. White t-shirts were a special prize. A good hit might leave a five-inch impact stain giving the impression they'd won a tie-dye contest. As I grew bigger, I spent a summer doing irrigation work on the same farm. This involved moving twelve-inch twenty-foot pipe across a corn field in knee deep mud. It seemed almost prophetic when we met the farmer at our new rental in July as he gave me a firm look before stating...

"Living on a farm is a lot different than working on one."

Quite the beginning after a brutal two-day drive in an overstuffed U-Haul under a hot sun. We'd got a late start, driving past the deep burning orange of a forest fire the first hour, before climbing the spine of Idaho at 25 miles per hour, pedal to the floor. The brakes squeaked, the load wobbled, and we barely crossed the state line into Washington by three in the morning. The following day, we reached the famed Portland traffic jam in the low light of the moon, making a final turn up old Hwy 221 by 11 p.m., changing our world forever. We woke up in the spare bedroom of the new landlord. A room tucked into the upstairs loft with bright, fresh towels surrounded by folk art. The morning sun revealed rough-hewn boards fastened together into a sliding door, once part of the homestead barn before it was made into living quarters.

We were anxious to unpack things, so chatted over coffee a few minutes before heading to the house to find our future. The previous renters trashed the home, leaving serious clean-up. The carpet crew were still rolling out the last few yards as we walked around them. The home was two stories with three bedrooms and a wood stove for winter. College students helped us carry the heavy furniture and boxes. By sundown of that first day, everything was in place. It was not only the closest I'd ever lived to a highway, it was my first electronic lock. The greatest selling point was an unobstructed view of Mount Hood.

My grandmother, born 1908, loved farm life. I remember her sharing the joy of getting an orange in her stocking each Christmas before opening her one gift. The world of the early twentieth century, in her words, created magic through everyday life. When the circus came to town, the entire crew would stroll down Main Street, parading acrobats, juggling clowns, and lumbering elephants. Papa, as she referred to him, often hosted railroad hobos or Native Americans at dinner during the Great Depression. She arose early one morning to watch Harry S. Truman make a campaign speech from the back of a train on his 1948 Whistle Stop Tour. Little pieces of her secret past came to light every now and again, prompted by something on an upper back shelf, or a small treasure deeply buried in a closet.

That is where I found a carefully wrapped ceramic tea pot, covered in layers of plastic, just behind my Doctor Doolittle puppet in the guest bedroom. I carried it out to the living room, certain it was some King Tut treasure (not to be violated without permission), placing it in her hands while looking on curiously.

Grandmother's Teapot

She examined it, searching her memory as I slid next to her on the couch. The plastic crinkled as she rolled down the first bag and her face glowed with a look of recognition. She clicked off her soap opera and began removing the remaining layers like an archaeologist revealing a sacred object at an ancient dig site. She smoothed each bag after removing it, then placed it on its predecessor. Slowly, a teapot shape emerged, a visible silver top and spout with a ceramic body of painted flowers. Once freed from the final bag, she held up the treasure to admire its floral design. She explained it was hand painted by relatives living outside of La Grande in the late 19th century.

Tugging open the lid, she slid in a hand, pulling free a faded piece of folded paper. She placed it in her lap before handing me the vessel, allowing my anticipation to build. She unfolded the wrinkled square until its secret was revealed. I leaned in, each new fold finally exposing these faded, handwritten words: *"This teapot was the only item to survive a family house fire in 1888."*

As we went on to experience the farm, I must admit, the farmer was right about farm life, but mostly about experiences that were unexpected. I already knew farms involved hard labor from dawn to dusk, but never suspected the degree of wildlife hiding in the nooks and crannies of the property. One of those unexpected surprises came from the single western red cedar that marks the boundary of the yard. It erupts into a stink bug colony early in the spring. The bark moves with their pale gray, slow moving bodies, but I could never learned why this tree held such singular importance among an orchard of trees. This is only the beginning of their full-fledged migration into our home. We find them crawling on our toothbrushes or in the soap dish. They cling to the curtains, cross the carpet, or hide in the closet. I once stepped on a poor fellow in the shower who blasted his stink scent while I was covered in soap. It took a few moments to figure out the pungent smell wasn't coming from the soap bar. They can be annoying, but never dangerous. In fact, most of the things living on the farm only become potentially dangerous when you act that way toward them.

Then there are the ladybugs. I opened the ancient and unused front door one winter to discover a favorite hibernation spot. There they were, a large red bundle, huddled together along the upper spine of the door. Once exposed to the interior, they'd mistake our evening fires for the warmth of spring and find their way into everything. This led to the most intense game of hide and seek I've ever played. When I was lucky enough to find one, I'd cup my hands around it, then attempt to skootch it toward my palm to toss it outside. Sadly, most went undiscovered, ending their lives dried up behind books, under furniture, or inside drawers. It can take months to clean them out each summer.

In the spring, the farm erupts in ribbits and croaks. It's become a ritual to stand at the front porch an hour after dark just to hear the wall of sound created by what resembles an amphibian happy hour. The sound is as forceful as an ocean wave, engulfing the listener like a dive into cold water. It is another aspect of nature's wonder inducing magic that goes mostly unnoticed by those racing by on the nearby highway. How joyful it has become to find one of it is to find one of our little neighbors by accident during the day, curled up in the petals of a rose, wedged in the leaf of a cornstalk, or dusted with pollen in the bell of a squash flower.

1 A.M.

Little armored wings

Flap like Japanese fans

In darkness…

Hovering, humming, wondering

What set them off this time?

Drift…slumber, then a descent

A dull thud gripping my face

GASP! Wake with a start!

Tarantula from the ceiling…?

Quick clutch grab

Toss to the wall-

Stink bug!

Again.

Occasionally an adult will hop in front of the car on a rainy night, causing me to endure a good soaking to move a turtle or frog rather than run over it. Appreciation and gratitude for nature opens pathways to beautiful worlds, attracting an unseen energy. Nature hides from those who yell at the top of their lungs on an isolated trail or carelessly destroy a bird's nest while changing the porch light.

There is one night on the farm I'll never forget. It was kind of a "Night of the Frogs" horror film, except this involved terminal cuteness hopping at you out of the darkness. It was 1:30 A.M., (often the magic hour on the farm), when I woke up on the couch, television blaring. I stumbled into the kitchen rubbing my eyes when the dog arrived, whimpering to be let out. He scampered off to his favorite spot before I noticed some twelve-to-twenty baby frogs, attracted by the warmth, hopping over the threshold into the house. I watched them in disbelief for a moment before attempting to interrupt their migration to herd them past the green popcorn machine and back towards the door. This had to be shared. My wife and I spent the next half hour tracking down each cute little Kermit until they were properly cupped and released from our warm hands into the garden. Only country life graces us with such unexpected moments.

There were other moments of course, such as the long-tailed weasel who ran across the yard in broad daylight, bobcats hunting a morning dove in the plum orchard, or the merlin falcon chick who chose to hide under a loose flap on the corner of the barn after falling from its nest. The worried parents continued to feed it to adulthood. Hoots from great horned owls and coyotes yips often fill our nights, but it is the type and variety of birds on the farm that are truly wonderous. In just two years, notable visitors included Cedar Waxwings, a Black Phoebe, a Lesser yellow legs, White Crowned Sparrows, Vesper sparrows, Yellow-rumped warblers, Common Yellow-throats, Song Sparrows, Western Bluebirds, Oregon Juncos, Great Blue Heron, American Kestrels, Red-Tailed Hawks, Northern Harriers, Bald Eagle, Cooper's Hawks, Killdeer, Canada Goose, Turkey Vultures, and Chipping Sparrows. Once the tractors are parked in the Fall, life stubbornly pushes its way back into the fields, waiting for that time when humans accept a partnership with the land over controlling it.

When the tractors are rolling, the farm is a freeway of activity. It was with an upcoming harvest of Italian plums our second season; the crew was short two members and I was asked to join the team for a few days. I'd worked on farms before, usually tossing hay bales or lining up irrigation lines, but I was never trusted to operate a tractor or harvester. I insisted on opening the storage barn a couple days early just so I could practice driving the tractor on the gravel road a few times. I really wasn't in the mood to kill myself for a few plums. My biggest worry was properly operating the forklift where the back of the machine was used to lift the large wooden crates after they were filled with fruit. As an operator, you had to effectively drive backwards while sliding each prong into the raised slot under the box before lifting to move it. Sounds easy, but when you're on a hill side with other machines moving around in the hot sun on the clock, it gets tricky. Sometimes, even a little dangerous. My job was to move filled boxes down slope to a flatbed trailer where another team loaded them into tidy rows.

When harvest day finally arrived, I showed up early in faded jeans and a pair of worn-out gloves in my back pocket. My old hay baling outfit. I would come to realize though, the most important equipment was the extra padding provided to place on the tractor seat. Working with a harvester and two other tractors took me a few hours before I fully synced with the team. It was almost a "dance", leaving empty crates ahead of the line before hauling off the full ones to the semi-truck below. As a rookie, I had to be careful to not over accelerate on corners heading downhill where I might tip over. There was also the risk of losing empty boxes with every bump on the gravel road if you didn't watch carefully to adjust. Large plum spills left between rows also presented a challenge. If you drove the downslope side of tractor wheels through them, the lubrication sometimes caused a sideways slide between two rows of trees rendering slippery tires useless under their own weight. With such a high learning curve it took a full day to function properly, finally feeling a little pride in my ability to adapt by day's end.

The main lesson of course, was even with all the machines and technology, farm life was still hard. It remained a year-round job filled with the roar of machines often extending far into the night. My choice many years before to turn away from this life for college made me feel the labor all the more powerfully in middle age. My frame seemed barely adequate to deal with the stresses. Still, there was a certain kind of joy that came from doing an honest days' work to feed people. As David Letterman used to say, it was a good kind of tired.

As with all of life, there was certainly sadness on the farm as well. My saddest moments came from battling mice when I seemed to have no alternative. They always had a cute naïve look on their face which made me want to like them, but they had the terrible habit of intentionally running through open doors trying to escape the cold only to nest behind the dishwasher. This caused problems in the form of chewed food bags during late night forays and irritating explorations over every inch of the house. One unfortunate fellow had a reflex jump off the side table after my wife reached for her alarm clock and he snapped right into the spring trap sitting below on the floor. In spite of evidence to the contrary, country mice are annoyingly smart, possessing an ability to elude live traps like little rodent Houdini's.

I've watched them skip over trap entrances to raid the dog food bowl and avoid precarious falls into bucket traps I'd constructed from online designs. They always found their way upstairs eventually, unable to resist our clothes, closets, and furniture leaving feces or damaged items. I hated the traditional snap traps, but once they exceeded our patience, we'd set them out. Surprisingly, even these would be licked clean of peanut butter or cream cheese without setting off the trigger, so I had to come up with a new system that left me feeling guilty. I'd set one trap packed with food in the middle of two other traps. That way they'd have to run over a scentless trap to get to the food. I absolutely hated being near the trap when one went off. I knew mice were only doing what they were programmed to do, and were incapable of being reasoned with as they never attended college or spoke English.

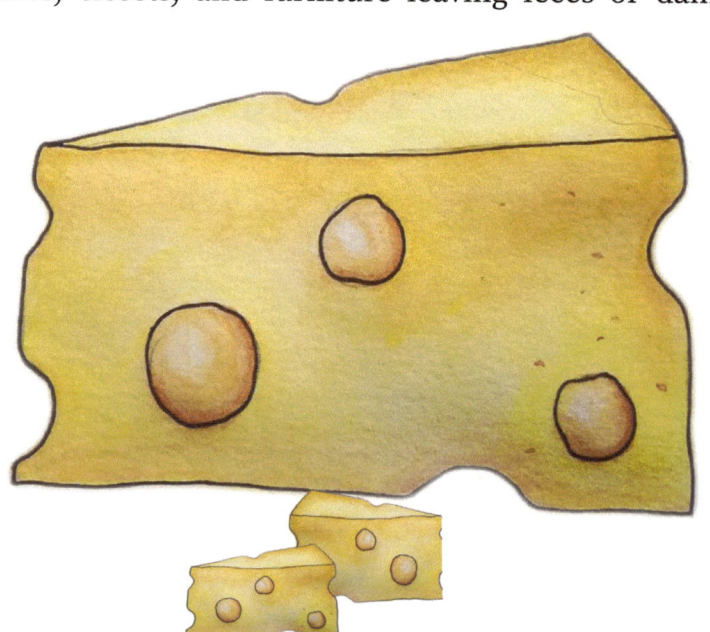

Still, with their deep shiny brown eyes and cuddly ears, I felt intensely sad each time that released bar signaled the end of another life.

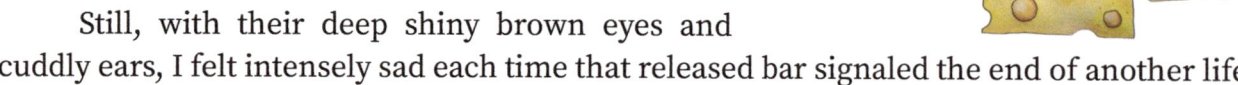

The Sum Total of a Mouse

Little mouse please forgive me,

For I took your life so thoughtlessly…

Picking a flower.

We placed you in the field

Buried among the leaves.

I feel your breath

In my memory.

Among the roses…

In ripening cherries…

Over the waterfall…

Upon the sun…

Across the bare field.

With heavy heart…

I set my trap.

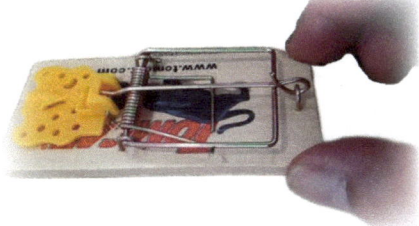

To end this chapter on a happier note, I'll share one positive memory of a mouse in our kitchen. There was one instance where a very troublesome fellow took the bait in our live trap. We came into the kitchen early that morning hearing tiny claws scrambling around the edges of the enclosed tin box searching for an exit. I was so relieved we wouldn't be burying another victim in the plum orchard, my wife and I dressed right away before heading to the pond a half mile up the gravel road, box in hand. There we found the thick briars of early spring just sending out their earliest shoots when I set down the box at the edge of the tangle. When I lifted the lid, there he was; alert and dead center, looking from my wife's eyes, to mine, then back again. Once he figured out mice were not on the breakfast menu, he jumped six inches into the air before scurrying off into the bramble. For once I was relieved; we both got what we wanted.

Heavenly Brushstrokes

Chapter 2

Childhood Through A Suburban Lens

"Taught to fear of Jesus in a small town."

-John Mellencamp

The life of a suburban kid in the 1960's was a new world in many ways. Computers that could fit on your lap were decades away while just about every other consumer gadget and gizmo ruled the day. We had a massive old wood stereo filled with dusty jazz records and a grainy radio that seemingly spewed magic and history. My brother and I listened to the Ali vs. Frazier fights on that radio, and the turntable played Glen Campbell Christmas albums complete with skips during the holidays. Christmas was the time to circle gift choices in the Sears catalogue, flock trees, and sip hot chocolate during Rudolf the Red-Nosed Reindeer. Dad and I put up the outside tree lights using his long broomstick from work with a nail driven through one end. I'd hold the line behind him so it would stay untangled as he'd raise each section far above his head into a zigzag pattern across the blue Tibetan Spruce on the corner. Some traditions went back decades, like exploring the contents of our stockings at 5 a.m. in front of the fireplace. Santa always left a note thanking us for the cookies while leaving nibbled carrot ends from his reindeer. The range of gifts was also impressive; my first bicycle, rock em' sock em' robots, pong, guitars, and steam puffing trains, among many others.

Marc and Kari Christmas guitars

Birthday zoo trip

Disneyland was on the agenda the summer I turned six. One of those famous cross-country trips we all endured as kids where parents lost their voices in the chaos of slap fights. We filled up our old green station wagon bomber, slept on dirty laundry, played license plate games, and told every joke we'd ever heard at school. Holiday Inns held the miracle of ice machines, and upon meeting the seven dwarfs, I found Sneezy, forever frozen mid-sneeze, scary! HE chased me around Cinderella's Castle until I'd shake his hand. Times were simpler, people were nicer, and I could walk the two blocks to a convenience store without being abducted.

My favorite time during summer though, were family visits to the country; we'd fish, hike, camp, and pause to celebrate life amidst the pine scented air. It was enough to just enjoy being alive. Dad led trips to Tam McCarther Rim from Three Creeks Lake years before they bothered making a trail. We'd follow without question, sliding along exposed slate, heads bobbing in a snaking line weaving through alpine fir. Gasping for breath, hands on our knees, losing sight of each other, then scampering to catch up before reaching the summit.

Family at Three Creeks

You knew you were in the heart of Oregon when the silence became so deafening your ears rang like warning bells. On the rim, we'd enjoy peanut butter and jelly sandwiches near a cool mist floating off the edge of a nearby snowbank. Dad decided when we'd rested enough. We'd follow him onto the giant bowl-shaped glacial cirque extending off the east rim of the cliffside. I would cautiously follow in the footprints he'd laid out across the steep embankment until it was decided we had gone far enough to launch. We'd stretch out our raincoats on top of the deep snow then jump on, quickly accelerating to a blazing speed. I was scared out of my wits, catching air from time-to-time, performing unintentional acrobatics. Down we'd go avoiding saplings and exposed rock until digging in our heels creating a spray of cold ice in our faces to stop. We smiled like it was fun, as admitting you were terrified while catching your breath just wasn't done in those days. Bravery was a high-prized commodity, as silly snow sliding was a fraction of the fear our uncles and granddads had faced in World War 2. Still, we were just kids.

Columbia Gorge Cliffs

Show No Fear

Line up shoulder to shoulder…

Largest to shortest,

oldest to youngest!

Zip up your coat,

wrap your neck,

pull up your boots.

A mountain calls,

danger lurks,

fear has no home.

Follow the leader.

Follow the sun.

Don't fall behind…

Run, climb, pant, slip on mossy shale…

Show no fear.

Be a man.

Hike the jagged rocks,

climb the desperate peak…

Pant the cool, misty wind.

Fear is a rumor.

While at home, life was also much different. Fast food was a rare once a month treat in our family. If we travelled to Portland or Salem, we'd go in as a family, treating fast food as a social family dinner rather than an emerging new lifestyle. I remember regretting the day McDonald's arrived in my hometown for the first time because I knew how easy it would be to turn to laziness in my daily food choices. The temptation of convenience was just too glaring. My placement at the tail end of the Baby Boomer generation put one foot in the letter writing culture of my youth and the other firmly in the Information Age. Computers began almost as a carnival curiosity in the beginning. My close friend Brian had followed the research and proudly showed me the metal box with a red light on top that turned on when he entered some code.

"What's the point? Does the red light give stock recommendations?" I asked as Brian looked on as if he were an early human explaining fire to a Neanderthal.

"The codes make the light turn on, it's neat." I took his word for it, but I saw no future in such an oddball invention. I'd purchase my first Apple computer while earning a Master's degree in 1994. I still remember how impressed I was with how my words and thoughts flowed out like water during those first few sessions of learning the Apple equivalent of Word.

Which of course brought me back to food, as I suddenly wasn't using liquid paper to correct every essay and found time to cook beyond tv dinners and canned chili. Though it took years to wean myself from the meat and potatoes American diet, I finally learned to trust my instincts and grow beyond my parents' sweet and sour chicken leftovers from the Dragon Gate Chinese restaurant.

It was a constant battle with my brother to get to them first, and there was nothing so disappointing as to be left holding an empty container late at night with only a few sad mushrooms in the corners.

At first, I found the sweetness only tolerable and the orange goo covering those breaded chicken pieces seemed like astronaut food, but it was my first training for what was to come.

"I didn't come this far...to only come this far"
-Jesse Itzler

What I miss most about growing up without fast food, or expensive sit-down restaurants, is the simple things. We pretty much did everything for ourselves with only a few ingredients. Fried bologna was certainly the easiest to make. You'd slice the circular meat piece at each quarter before flopping it in a frying pan on medium heat. Each flap would curl upward as it started to sizzle, and there was nothing quite like placing it on toasted white bread with yellow mustard. The equivalent of today's COSTCO hotdog. Tang, green Jell-O, Kool Aid, Tropical Hawaiian Punch, Strawberry Quik, and popcorn were all easy fixes for a kid, and the messes left behind were

easy to clean up, making for a happier mom. In our household, Friday was popcorn night. This preceded the power line-up of The Mary Tyler Moore Show, The Bob Newhart Show, and The Carol Burnett Show. Even when my older siblings reached their seventies party years, it kept its place in the family pantheon. It was that one moment during the week, beyond the dinner table, where we gathered as a family to relax, laugh, and sort through problems. We only had the "Big Three" television stations at that time, and for some reason, I'd always wake up on the couch with dad snoring while holding a half full beer on his chest. SCTV (Canadian Television comedy) was always in its final few sketches as I clicked off the set and poked dad with a finger. Bedtime. I watched the very first Saturday Night Live on that couch, and to my memory, the cast was much more fearless and daring in its drug focused bombastic sketches that favored improvisation over cue card reading. Chevy Chase mastered the pratfall and fake news that first season, while the audience endured ridiculous headlines under their chin before each break, such as, "Thinking of eggnog in spring." Crazy times of disco and unity emerged.

Mike at sister's birthday party.

My first exposure to young girls outside of the classroom was the McMinnville Skating Rink. It was a beat-up old remnant from the 50's painted in mental institution green holding a skating floor of thin oak slats covering a large oval. Skates were rented next to the snack bar where we'd sit on wooden benches convinced each skate would only make it past the ankle if we grunted loud enough. We'd shakily enter the skating round, attempting a series of straight lines before mastering the circle. I'd consider the venture a success if I managed to avoid plowing into a group of sixth graders holding ice slushies. But the most tension an eleven year old boy could face at the time came once the box board lit up on the wall announcing, "Girls' Choice Skate" from a list of

DJ selected options. The girl's choice line sent every pre-teen boy into a frantic run for the boy's bathroom for sanctuary. The laughter in our safe place was infectious, feeling we'd pulled one over on our feminine pursuers. Revenge would be sweet a few years later however, when the most terrifying psychosis ever was being rejected for a dance at the Spring May Day event. No one actually believed females had cooties of course, but we did know if you held a girl's hand for the duration of one song at age eleven, blushing your rear end off, you'd never hear the end of it from your friends at school.

Grandfather in 1920's

On weekends I'd often go exploring as wilderness started abruptly across the street just behind our home. Baker Creek meandered its way along the northern town boundary, finding a path through oak groves and shrubs before dancing through local farmland. I learned from a neighborhood boy that if you took a hunk of liver, tied it to a string before tossing it out in a large pool of water, you could catch river lobster. Not actual lobster, but the crawfish found within walking distance of my home were so immense, the claws were big enough to cook and eat AS lobster. I'd request liver, which I hated, for lunch just so I'd have leftovers I could bring along with a bucket and a fishing net for my endeavors. I'd search for a suitably shaded pool, with sun illuminating the edges,

where I might lure my prey into the shallow water. A few hard lessons, through trial and error, taught me to pull the string slowly toward me after the diners got their first taste of meat. If the string were jerked, a flick of the tail was all I'd catch before they'd dash back into the deeper water. It was also key to place the net into the shallows beforehand as stabbing the surface once they were close was never fast enough to fool their acute senses. When I found a successful routine, I'd usually bring home my bucket filled with three or four of the critters to release into a three-foot kiddie pool. There I'd watch them move around for hours until I figured out the chlorine wasn't good for their health. From then on, I'd load them back in the bucket after a couple hours for release into the shady pool where I'd found them. I'm sure their little brains wondered who that mad scientist kid was that abducted them for study.

Neskowin Beach State Park

I always observed and studied things as a child. Just as my mom, as a small child, would sit next to animals her father trapped or shot in Eastern Oregon, studying them for hours; I'd fill my shelves with unusual rocks, bottle caps, or model airplanes. Becoming a collector evolved from being a shy kid who steered clear of groups and potential antagonists. I even kept the leftovers from a family dinner once, just to study the structure of a salmon skeleton as it decomposed on my bookshelf. I suspect that's why I was so attracted to the big bones of dinosaurs and the fantasies of life during the cretaceous age. A little child without much power in a world of adults will learn how to avoid being noticed by hiding his green beans in his milk carton, or float away into a dream where he can't be touched. Being lost in that world eventually led to adventures in the real one. A healthy progression toward adulthood.

Although I never ran for class president or took a meaty role in a school play, I found I more than made up for such things by having a healthy awareness of my sense of place, and the crazy goofball people who chose to fill it. Whether floating out to observe breeching gray whales on migration to Alaska near Depot Bay or driving two hours into Eugene to try the vegan cornbread at the Cornbread Café, my life in Oregon has always been one based on adventure. The payoff is life.

Chapter 3

A Culinary Adventure

"Sometimes you just need to go off
the grid and get your soul right."
-LiveLiveHappy.com

I doubt Oregon invented them, or can even claim the highest number per capita, but food cart culture certainly has attained the status of an art form within the Willamette Valley. This underdog longshot came from humble origins when people took small pull trailers and converted them into kitchens. There are still remnants of these first few pioneers easily spotted by the holes sawed into their side wall for customers to order at as chefs turned onions in their makeshift kitchens. But the very first mobile food units I recall, were low-profile trucks with stainless steel storage areas that lifted up at the sides to reveal their Willy Wonka interior. One always showed up for my fourth-grade little league games, cleaning up with candy bar and nacho orders. The idea has since expanded into an economic powerhouse and become fertile ground for culinary adventures even across socio-economic lines. Recently, the trend developed toward higher tech kitchens as high start-up costs and limited space left graduating chefs little alternative. The food cart was a late bloomer in many ways, but soon became the primary outlet for chefs waiting on phone calls offering them the chance to produce their culinary magic. Suddenly it was a very competitive market, and they grew at light speed, becoming the substitute alternate choice over walled restaurants. Menu options range from Caribbean spicy ribs to vegetarian crepes.

Food Cart in St. Johns

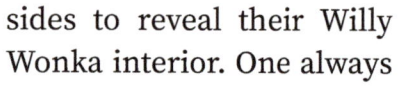

The wondrous side-effect of being a "foodie" is I've developed right alongside this trending explosion. When the urge suits me, I can visit pretty much any food in the world without putting a hole in my pocket. Old favorites often get a facelift with the new fusion trend popular in many cities now, but it's the people that really give a visit that adventurous spice. I might find a

Fish and Chips Food Truck in Nehalem

culinary arts student working to pay off loans, or, as with one recent encounter, a sweet mother from Nicaragua running the Tre' Bros cart just off the coast near Warrington. Personalities can be just as tasty as the food, and I'm sure standing in a ten by four space all day can make even the saltiest chef a little friendlier. Yadira was anything but salty, as she readily recommended the grilled shrimp tacos right after discussing her hibernating potted plants, and the Nicaraguan specialty of cerviche. The tacos were excellent, and my mother loved the lime, cilantro, shrimp combo in her mix. As with most of my favorite finds, I happened upon Tre' Bros by chance, a brilliant accident after a wrong turn on my way to Home Depot. An exciting mistake for a true hobbyist.

Many other food adventures come from "best of" categories that pop up on my computer when I check social media. The lists are for things like Best Diner or Best Pancakes for each state in the specific category. Oregon standouts usually land in Portland, but occasionally Bend or Eugene will snag something like Best Romantic Dinner or Best Cornbread. Still, my best finds happen by chance; I'll spot a new food cart on the edge of a parking lot, commit it to memory, and return later when time allows. That's how I found Recess in Tillamook, Le Camel in Sellwood, and Flourish in St. Johns.

From the state list, my most recent conquest was in the Best Italian category. Italian food was such a staple in American homes during my childhood that it will forever be associated with warm spaghetti and garlic toast steaming between our smiling faces. It was just too tempting a comfort food category to pass up. Even though I've expanded my food palate significantly since growing up, once I read the Italian winner was a food cart called Gumba in NE Portland, I planned out my trip like a giggling mad scientist. The drive to NE Alberta Street was doable, and Gumba featured a rotating menu with a panache' for presentation and contrasting flavors. We all know about hobbies, once you're hooked, you crave new experiences with a passion. So it was, I ditched a pile of paperwork a week later and surrendered to my dreams of handmade pasta. It was just dumb luck my hobby coincided with Portland rising to the status of "food city" with many critics during my absence.

The Bow Picker in Astoria

Driving holds its own challenges near Portland, as it has become a bit of a traffic tangle, but with some determination, I reached the off ramp leaving the rumble of congestion behind. Alberta Street is a charming area where a kid on a bicycle will still say hello to you while passing on the sidewalk. Following the Google Map voice, I turned by a food pod complex near 16th avenue to park thinking I'd found my target. However, after a short walk I was left confused. There were only shuttered BBQ and Mexican places surrounding a small parking lot. Google indicated I was off by a couple of blocks, so I took my time strolling by community businesses. It was a hot, sunny June day, so walking was invigorating. It turned out the site was tucked into a U-shaped mall and so unassuming I nearly passed it in stride. A quick squint revealed the famous food cart was riding out the pandemic in an interior space with only a dull blue neon sign to guide the unfamiliar. I strolled in filled with anticipation, finding the chef already sorting vegetables on his grill as the waitress yawned an unimpressed stare at my tattered jeans. I didn't take offense, as I also wore my usual tasting uniform of unassuming t-shirt and faded baseball cap. I confessed right up front I'd never been in before. I told her I'd appreciate any recommendations that would highlight the Best Italian title while giving me a good sampling of the chef's skill.

After narrowing her eyes and stroking her chin, she recommended the Pappardelle Pasta with a braised beef for $15, but I no longer ate beef, so I greedily eyed the steelhead instead. After ordering, I lounged in the tiny courtyard enjoying a coffee photo shoot (so Portland) during the interim. My number 10 hockey puck went ballistic after 20 minutes and there I sat with a well folded bag and a cup of cold water. I have been to Italy three times in my life, but I can only think of one other dish I enjoyed so thoroughly.

Within the bag were two cut sections of fish filled with a special stuffing coated with breadcrumbs, laid on a bed of mixed fluffy potatoes. The chef poured a special orange hot sauce over the entire dish before adding a sweet barbeque sauce as a final touch in the small oven. Some greenery provided a final flair before the pie tin was capped and served. My first bite, including a fin, seemed to last for an eternity as I enjoyed the contrasting hot, sweet, salmon flavor rainbow. Finally, here was a dish competing in the big leagues, but affordable to the masses. The world disappeared for 18 minutes as I savored every last enjoyable bite. Here was the reason I lived near Portland, here was the reason I drove two hours for the experience of food.

As luck would have it, the hot sun lay low in the sky as I scooped my final bites filled with a renewed vigor for adventure. I'd tossed in a wonderful little book titled, Walk There, a few moments before leaving, which proved a great stroke of luck. I carefully placed it under an arm before locking the car and perusing its pages. The air had finally cooled enough for me to indulge another favorite Oregon hobby, walking.

*More Flavor...***Le Camel**: A happy Middle Eastern accident while visiting Cap Cloud Puzzles in Sellwood for Christmas gifts. Another reason to keep my puzzle habit.

Recess: A small trailer in a gravelly parking lot next to the Killer Bean in Tillamook. I watched staff inside rolling balls of dough for their burger buns one evening and had to stop for a taste. Great burgers, awesome fries, love the Recess sauce.

Flourish: A cozy food truck at the St. Johns Food and Beer Porch. Amazing vegan cuisine for those who might never touch it. It was my wife's order of chicken parm that really wowed me. A broad assortment of other options to explore and compare. True food adventure.

Chapter 4

Exploring

"Difficult roads often lead to
beautiful destinations."
-Unknown

George Fox University

I've always loved walking, and living in four different states over a twenty-year period (Oregon, Arizona, Michigan, and Montana) only grew my love for experiencing new foods, whiteout blizzards, driving thunderstorms, and inner-city skylines. Every city, every landscape, is worth exploring if you see the people, their sense of place, and the vibrant interactive community as a whole. Gardens and bricks fill up the space between us of course, but the wear of time and history give a distinct personality to each stretch of real estate. I've held on to my favorites since childhood, continuing to visit sacred spots well into my fifties, even learning how the dimensions of light and season influence feelings and perceptions of landscape. I might enjoy the geology contained within a garden wall, or the way it casts a foreboding shadow when bathed in snow and a surreal winter light. A walk of quiet solitude engages everything wonderful about being human and an appreciation for earthly wonder. These seeds of reflection leave a lingering promise for more.

Lewis & Clark State Park

Oregon is a remarkable walking state, and I am the Lizzy Bennet of Oregon walks. Though my knees have begun their long serenade toward uselessness in screaming pain, I will continue to amble down backstreets and mountain passes until I am only left with memories in these old bones. There is friendship and warmth in landscape. Whether the taste of air, or the feelings evoked by an old oak in spring, I walk until I am absorbed into the composition of place. Passing cars ask me for directions as I seem to belong, becoming another piece of the jigsaw for this particular neighborhood.

After my experience at Gumba, I was ready to wander. Glancing at the tiny map contained within the book gave pause near the colorful Community Biking Center. I took a photo, reminded of the group I had met there years before. I then followed 14th Avenue south to pick up the route on NE Going where I found wondrous dogwood trees decorating the sky with starry blooms. One home had a beautiful, rounded staircase descending to the sidewalk, inspiring a daydream for all the community conversations once held there. The spot feels as if it is haunted by history. I walk the boundary of King Park before

cutting across a dry grassy school yard to catch 9th running near the Common Bond Garden where I find a large white tent containing a wedding reception. The attendees gawk at me blankly like a zoo bus passing the elephants when a woman seizes the microphone to tell her story.

"So, I must have been five years old that night when the banging on the front door began. Mama said, KIDS! Grab some knives and get in here! Each brother and sister ran in with an appropriately large knife gleaming from the surreal streetlamp light entering our side windows. We stabbed into the wood just behind the quaking door hopeful if the lock broke, the knives would hold whoever, or whatever wanted in. Just then, mama yelled, if that lock goes, get me my shotgun!"

House with unique steps off Alberta

I am reminded of why I walk cities. The odd personalities, the random encounters, the kids jumping bikes off poorly constructed plywood, the street person grumbling to himself about trains, the waitress filling saltshakers at 5 a.m. A different kind of texture from that found at the pond during my early morning meditations on the farm, but then, Oregon is alive with texture. The smell of gritty, sandy earth filled with pebbles along the bank of her streams, the rugged feel of Ponderosa Pine bark on the back as one leans against it to tug on a shoe in July. Texture appeals to my artist's eye which strives to see the guts in all things. Walking in Tillamook, I remember the sound of tennis shoes scrapping hot pavement as two ten-year-old's jogged past, lost in conversation. Or how the smooth, rounded basalt stones glistened a dull black before clicking together in a mass volcanic symphony as Pacific waves attempted to draw them back to the sea at Ecola State Park. I've absorbed these stories and they have left an indelible mark. Walking Oregon is so much more than exercise, it is a lifestyle.

Dogwood trees near Alberta Street

It was an early Sunday morning when I dropped my wife off at the airport and decided to head south on 82nd Ave to enjoy the city. Catching Portland sleeping in the spring is such a rarity for me, I drove by a few favorite spots before walking Barley. Soon, I found myself heading west on Alberta Street taking full advantage of the quiet to watch early morning joggers and businesses opening their doors. This end of things told the tale of the past two years, with boarded up store fronts covered by graffiti and the occasional bundled up homeless person. Then suddenly, I was in familiar territory. I pulled over next to the Community Cycling Center for a stretch and a quick look at the neighborhood. I walked right into the middle of the street before gazing east, then west. Not a soul. A few minutes after 6 a.m. I felt like a character in Stephen King's *The Stand*. I took the opportunity to walk over to the Cycling Center and take a close look at the colorful art covering the west wall. With the usual bustle, a few undisturbed seconds was all I could usually hope for, but today, the art, as well as that across the street came to life and was filled with hope. Community joy is how I might describe it. I was grateful for that "secret power" often held within the spell of a mural, and the curious mind prone to explore such places.

Alberta Community Cycling Center

"I am but a tourist

as the Ruddy Ducks dive and

wave webbed feet

at the sky."

The Crystal Springs Rhododendron Garden

When I arrive after an absence of decades, I find the parking lot below filled with anxious, young men stretching into wet suits, balancing surf boards on their heads pointed at the sea. The secret spots of my childhood are popular now, but somehow, Ecola State Park continues to hold a sacred spirituality. It is whispered through the white crested waves passing stone monuments in rank. Bubbling battalions, reaching for land, rolling up the shore. Unaware rock hounds and children are sent running, sliding over worn cobbles and colorful gravels until the water finally subsides and percolates into the sand. There, the ocean grabs hold, before pulling at the land with such force the stones rattle and roll like a tambourine band. I climb atop a boulder. The chaos below crashes around me with ferocity until I hear the house band play its familiar song.

Ecola State Park south of Seaside.

Bagels and books on Broadway before wandering through the Irvington neighborhood.

Four eye-catching homes in the Irvington neighborhood off Broadway.

Statues

Joan of Arc statue in Portland
dedicated on Memorial Day, May 30, 1925

Mastodon statue near wetlands where remains
were found in Tualatin

Statues serve the same function as an exclamation point serves in a sentence. POW! This is what our community stands for, likes to think it stands for, WANTS to stand for, or commissioned an artist to make others think it's what we stand for. Whatever the motivation, statues always draw my attention when I happen into one. I tend to move around them observing how light and design impact the shape from differing angles. A well thought out statue may be enjoyed on many levels. First and foremost, they are best experienced as a piece of art, but may also extoll a specific moment in history, be a tribute to someone or something, communicate concepts such as abstract or classical, represent the anger of a people or protest, and speak to the skill of the artist. I would place the Statue of Liberty and Mount Rushmore in a completely different category of course, but they are not in my state. I am often surprised by how few of my fellow pedestrians stop to enjoy them the way I do.

State Capitol sculpture in Salem

It is the randomly discovered statue that lights my curiosity most deeply. It is these surprise encounters that provide the exclamation point or yellow high-lighter within my ordinary daily experience. In the spirit of that find, all the statue photos I've included were secondary encounters that occurred while on my way to someplace else. Although, I am aware of many of their locations, such as the layered sitting lady in Lake Oswego, I only made one special trip to visit a statue during my writing. That was the gold Joan of Arc statue in East Portland, impressive in her determined elegance at the center of a city roundabout. I stopped to park just off the traffic circle before Barley and I walked half of the perimeter admiring the setting. We then explored the beautiful neighborhood surrounding her kingdom.

Capitol sculpture

Linfield University statues

Salem Rooster

Head sculpture at OHSU medical in Portland

Winged armour statue in Salem

Statue in Lake Oswego

Fall dragon statue in Newberg

Another interesting Salem statue

Museums

I am from a breed of people, who upon travelling to a new place, it has become second nature to look up museums and places of interest. This ingrained skill has led me to such travelling conquests as the Leonardo Di Vinci horse in Grand Rapids, Michigan, the Dali Museum in Orlando, Florida, and the City Library of Seattle with its bizarre portrait of tentacles coming out of bookshelves. I'm a museum hound and I will sniff out your cities' Houdini handcuffs, large ball of twine, or hidden murals within a matter of hours. I think my passion began with a trip to the Smithsonian in Washington D.C., tagging along with my uncle. It was the summer before my 8th grade year and social media was yet to be a thing. In just a few hours I located the Hope Diamond, the Wright Brothers first powered airplane, and George Washington's false teeth. Or maybe it was the King Tut exhibit of 1976 that got me hooked. It had been touring in celebration of the American Centennial, and the entire atmosphere surrounding the event was absolute magic.

It would be years later while working on an education degree at Lewis and Clark College, I had the pleasure of spending a summer at the Oregon Museum of Science and Industry in Portland. Its original site next to the Portland Zoo was a childhood Mecca. It had been filled with such oddities as the transparent woman, whose organs lit up as the assembled fourth graders gawked open-mouthed. Chief Leluska was another powerful memory.

Leonardo Di Vinci horse in Grand Rapids, Michigan

Octupus Mural at the City Library in Seattle, WA

Native Americans wearing striking carved cedar masks danced the legends of their people as the old chief, wrapped in a red blanket, narrated. By the summer of my employment, the museum had moved east across the Willamette River to the hipper side of Portland. I would take the floor during the tour of automated dinosaurs, who roared and moved, as small children hid behind their mothers. More recently, I returned to the museum for an exhibit of King Tut Replicas that were so convincing and stunning, I felt that twinge of excitement I experienced 45 years before. Much of the exhibit had the artifacts placed together as they'd been originally found, stacked in replica rooms of the tomb, giving the

Queen Nefertari exhibit at the Portland Art Museum

King Tut replicas at Oregon Museum of Science and Industry in Portland

Willamette Heritage Museum in Salem

Textile machine

Early home in Salem - part of Willamette Heritage Site

Textile machine

Textile machine

Howard Carter (archaeologist) perspective.

Although I have never been a person particularly enamored with stuff, there are two exceptions in my life: books and museum gift shops. I still own a replica terracotta Chinese warrior from the Portland Art Museum exhibit I toured years ago. I also have rolled up artwork from their Monet exhibit, as well items from the High Desert Museum in Bend, and lingam stones from the Rice Northwest Museum of Rocks & Minerals in Hillsboro. I tend to see museum gift shops the way most people view a garage sale. My refrigerator has become somewhat of a tribute to them. The front and sides are covered in colorful magnets I've collected from every stop. At this rate, I will need a new refrigerator in under three years.

"Oregon holds answers to questions we have not yet learned to ask."

-Unknown

Aurora Community Museum

The Depot Museum in Canby

Flavel House Museum in Astoria

Astoria Art Museum

The World's Oldest Shoes, NHM in Eugene

Natural History Museum in Eugene

(the above 3 photos) Dali Museum

Brain cell and Godzilla's earring at the Frederik Meijer Garden & Sculpture Park, Grand Rapids, MI

Prehistoric Gardens

" The Museum is not meant either for the wanderer to see by accident or for the pilgrim to see with awe. It is meant for the mere slave of a routine of self- education to stuff himself with every sort of incongruous intellectual food in one indigestible meal."

-Gilbert K. Chesterton

Chapter 5

Walking With Curiosity

"In every walk with nature one
receives far more than he seeks."
-John Muir

Bridges

Bridges are one of those inventions that seem to reinvent themselves every historic age in spite of what appears to be such a dreary function, getting us over things. Most see them as an afterthought, if considered at all, but I've always found them worthy of examination. The first time I saw the Brooklyn Bridge and The Golden Gate Bridge in San Francisco, I was held in breathless wonder as a child. I am unable to separate my experiences in those cities from the beautiful bridges that served as their backdrop. While I am more of a nature person than an industrialist, there is still something in those architectural achievements and their historic legacy that make me slow my step as I cross over them. Even the newer footbridges reflect new technologies and aesthetic choices which stamp a certain magic as the postmark to our passing. Somewhere in time, Oregon became an interesting bridge state for me. I've even planned a few day trips around them. Some represent engineering achievements, such as the Tillicum Bridge in Portland, while others give you a window into the idyllic age of our grandparents such as the covered bridges around Cottage Grove. I've decided that bridges do far more than get you across, they represent a vital link between cultures, the life blood in our economic veins, and the genius of designers like Brooklyn Bridge architect James Kirby. So, take your time while in Oregon to walk a little further. Smell the roses, then cross a bridge.

Newport Bridge

Salem Bridge

Covered bridge near Cottage Grove

St. Mary's Bridge near Portland

Crossing St. Mary's Bridge

Astoria bridge into Washington

Crossing Newport Bridge

George Fox campus bridge

Portland Bridge

Salem Footbridge

Trains

It wasn't a far step from watching my brother set up his 1969 train set, with real puffing steam, to rushing toward a long stretch of isolated railroad tracks near my Great Uncle's farm once the ground began to rumble. Every time a long, heavy train hummed off in the distance, I'd run with my father, holding his hand, to watch boxcars clack over the seams in the track. I dreamed of riding the rails like a hobo, waving at onlookers as I pondered where to jump off for a fishing trip or deep woods hike. To this day, whenever I see an old steam engine rusting along the roadside or sitting in a museum, it evokes powerful visions connected to my childhood. Every now and again, I'll venture a climb. I'll see an old behemoth sitting in a park and I'll think about the meaning of freedom touching its cold skin. Stoking the boiler fire before pulling the whistle cord, I watch the landscape of a continent pass me by with a humming smile. I am intrigued by powerful machines pulling miles of swaying boxcars between Seattle and Maine; the cares of reality shed like leaves out the open side windows. Metal pounding in circles powered by steam is so far removed from the passive rhythm of my windshield wipers.

Georgia Pacific in Corvallis

Engine 25 in Wheeler

It was a crisp Fall morning when my brother and I left mom's house just South of Canon Beach. He was unusually quiet as he gazed out the passenger window while we passed through Wheeler. As fate would have it, there sat a coal black steam engine on the tracks, belching white steam like a factory, similar to the one circling our living room so many Christmases ago. Both of us did a double, double take, believing we'd crossed some twilight zone portal to our twentieth century childhood. Catching myself in mid-daydream, I turned the steering wheel with such force we skidded onto the gravel shoulder as my door flew open the moment we came to rest. I was open-mouthed, smiling as I descended the small embankment to observe the great beast. Why was it here? Why had a

Train in Corvallis

crowd failed to gather? Were we the only ones with toy train childhoods? I began snapping photos with my cell as it struck me why expensive cameras had lined the waterway the last mile of our drive, train paparazzi! They lay in wait for old steam engines just as Hollywood paparazzi wait for a Kardashian to emerge from the hospital with a newborn baby. If you've ever walked around one of those art shows in the park, you'll know there exists people who blow up photos of trains to make a living off them. They set up their tripods across the country, waiting for trains in various weather conditions, just as nature paparazzi, who take nature photos for hunting magazines, lay in wait for elk with wildflowers stuck in their antlers. Although I may never possess the photographic talent to be a true paparazzi, I feel the experience was pretty much my first train stalking. I am hooked, and will never fail to pull over for a steaming lively boiler, or a rusted-out pile of metal that once held greatness, now covered with children climbing over it with the glint of an adventurer's eye.

Not long ago, while investigating Tillicum Bridge in Portland, I noticed there was a new train center being assembled in the Southeast section of the city. I could only look through the cyclone fence at the time as it had yet to open, but I was grateful knowing people exist like me who believe these monster metal horses deserve their place in history as well as a respectful place of rest in retirement.

Model trains in Portland

Engine 25 in Wheeler

Old rail house in Cottage Grove

Engine 25 in Wheeler

Sunsets & Waterfalls

Sunsets and waterfalls are perhaps the purest of joys of my life, and Oregon has been blessed with large doses of both. I'll count dawn as a sunset, because it is basically the same thing in reverse, leading to the same inability to capture in words, painting, or photo, their truly spectacular nature. Tourists visiting the coast have even taken to the Hawaiian practice of dropping everything at sunset to head to the waterfront to observe the last rays of a plunging sun. It is the one time in our hectic day of rushing that all of us can reside in that one moment of peace we so desperately crave. When I've stayed with my mother atop her small coastal hilltop, I've taken to joining them, although, I've been addicted since childhood. The vine covered hills block my view on the farm, leaving me feeling a bit short changed. For me, sunsets and waterfalls represent a kind of natural power that recharges and invigorates the soul, drawing the individual like a moth to flame. Just as I struggled to see the passing comet Neowise, or the 2018 full eclipse in Oregon, there is an excitement fused with energy.

Maybe it's my natural compass, or perhaps a favorite fairytale, but when my wife and I came across a waterfall about 100 feet off a major freeway twenty years ago, we gained a new perspective. It was such a visible spot, that fifty some onlookers stopped with the same idea, jumping out to spend a few minutes walking around, take a quick photo, then settle back on the highway. Soon though, it became clear that something was missing in that space normally occupied by waterfall energy. The natural rhythms no longer seemed to chime with the sun and its mesmerizing chorus.

The falls remained beautiful, and the water roared as elsewhere, but something had been removed, like the heart from a breathing organism. The waterfall still held the characteristics of

a special place, but that magic spiritualism that had always been such a part of the experience was drained away. Almost as if a large bathtub spigot were closed. I had to walk around the site, seeing it from different angles while watching the crowd mill through the shrubs, to gain an understanding. When I crouched near the ground, I noticed the closeness of the road meant easy access for thousands that led to a mass trampling of the habitat. Almost as if a sizable herd of elephants had passed. An unconscious wandering that had robbed the site of much of its vigor. That's why we should never consider putting roller coasters on mountain tops, or turn the moon into a scarred, ragged mining camp. Such exploitation takes more than minerals, it sucks the life force out of beautiful places important to our mental health and lands a blow to the future peace of mind for others.

I once attended an environmental seminar where an older gentleman shared a tragic story about his brother. He was one of those people that held a deep connection with the environment and found our cultural need to exploit forest and landscape for consumer goods a destructive wrong. As the story goes, one day he shared this love of wilderness with a man who saw things differently. "You can't eat a tree" the man said bluntly, a statement that drove so deeply into the psyche of the brother that it troubled him for years. He had no answer for the appetite of our monied system, and eventually succumbed to suicide over continuing to live with that realization.

I was inspired to lift up that torch and reflect on an answer, "why was wilderness equally important to the board feet demanded by our culture?" After much thought, I arrived at my conclusion. You may indeed not be able to eat a tree, but you will never be able to buy peace of mind.

"You and I are all as much continuous with the physical universe as a wave is continuous with the ocean."
-Alan Watts

Silverfalls near Salem

My Journals

Multnomah Falls

White River Falls near Dufur

Colummbia Gorge waterfall

The Joy of a Random Waterfall

The rains had let themselves known for a week, when an unexpected day of sun was forecast for the upcoming Tuesday. My wife was excited and declared since I was *the one who always investigated things,* it would be *my job* to find something outdoorsy to do with the dog that day. I visited a few forest service sites, some event calendars, then did a waterfall search for the Willamette Valley. When I saw photos and reviews for McDowell Creek Park, I was intrigued by the large wooden stair complex that led to a viewing platform, and I just had to know. There were only a couple of parking spots remaining by the time we arrived, but the journey had been a memorable one. We were both soaked in sweat, covered in mud, and survived many descending slippery mud stairs. What really struck me in that moment, however, was how many amazing, isolated waterfalls I have yet to see. The beauty of Oregon is that on any day, with a little effort, you are more than likely within driving distance of something special. I regret I have but one short life to experience it all.

"Grace is finding a waterfall when you were only looking for a stream.
-Vanessa Hunt

Rust In Peace

I can't say when I became attracted to old rusty things, but sometime between attending college at Michigan State University and doing salvage archaeology in Arizona, I became enamored with old, abandoned antiques. Walking transit lines, looking at stone, I'd come across the occasional model T riddled with bullets abandoned in the scrub, or forgotten mining equipment twisted at the bottom of a gully. When I stepped near or over these items it would immediately trigger an inner curiosity. Suddenly I began to formulate questions in my mind. *Who were these people that made a life out of these old, rusty things? What compelled them to drop everything and take the next train to Chicago?*

Tractor mailbox near Amity

Within every rusty thing there resides a mystery. I suppose the Second World War, or the Great Depression would have been sufficient reason to drop everything, or possibly a copper vein pursued deep into the earth finally petering out. When I see a pair of rusty railroad tracks curving off into the distance, I want to follow them to their source. Something about releasing all cares to my inner hobo I find appealing. A silent revolt for freedom. A last stand against daily traffic jams and burnt espressos. I think something inside all of us yearns for simpler times, explaining why so many drag that antique farm plow into their front yard only to hang a mailbox on it. Perhaps this is also what drives the artist to hammer out a sculpture from the twisted remains of a garbage pile. I've rediscovered Oregon seeing the personality of forgotten things.

Abandoned former lives lay everywhere across the state, but perhaps my favorite resides just outside Corvallis, time warping to that place in history where farming was king. It was in the first part of the twentieth century when Thompson's Mills Heritage Site was full throttle grinding and bagging flour.

Thompson's Mills Heritage Site

Thompson's Mills

Thompson's Mills Heritage Site printing plates

When you first see the reflection of the silos in the mill pond, that are so well preserved, you expect to see men in hats and well-worn overalls carrying out heavy sacks to idling Model-Ts. It certainly isn't isolated in the middle of nowhere, but there are still plenty of old rusty things to go around. Just inside the entrance there sits a pile of rusty gears enticing visitors to take the tour. The old floorboards creak while your eyes adjust, and the site caretaker puts down her pen to offer a tour. Only in an old flour mill would another couple arrive, exchanging a colorful parrot between their shoulders, to complete our group. Something about old museums and rusty metal seems to attract eclectic oddballs like myself. Maybe I watched too many pirate movies as a kid, but I swear that bird stared me down the entire time. I particularly enjoyed the printing plates for the different ground products spread across the floor. I would wallpaper my living room with these vintage drawings if they allowed me too.

After feeding the circling fish some cracked corn through a small window facing the stream, we descend a cramped set of wooden stairs that lead into the guts of the place. Our leader carefully guides our heads past obstacles that caused bumps and bruises on many an unwary worker in the past. I'm guessing early twentieth century workers were much shorter too. Just in front of us, the guide flicks on a switch. This instantly brings drooping belts and a large spinning wheel to life. I can't even imagine working amidst such noise every day while bagging feed, but there is still something charming about the simpler lives lived by our grandparents.

A few hours away in the central Oregon city of Bend, you may see another of my favorites. Along the Deschutes River walk, the city created a monument to early logging culture by making an artistic statue from rusty metal bent and welded into form. Two draft horses pull a large, beautiful representation of a Ponderosa Pine log, with very strange contents within. Some of the original antique chainsaws from the area fill the interior space. Not the short-nosed ones we use today, but long hefty ones with heavy chains extending some four or five feet from the engine. I'm certainly more of a hiking enthusiast than a clearcut fan, but this tribute in particular pulls off that rare find of making a piece of art from metal while communicating the daily struggle of those who came first. It speaks of the early pioneer lifestyle with no need of words. It really shows the energy required to settle a state.

Of course, most of my favorite discoveries continue to be those abandoned cars left in the middle of a field, or under the shade of a Douglas Fir tree. These rusty relics are different from the cars you see littering front lawns in rural communities today, as they appear to be left in the exact spot where they gave out while working in a field or died after being carefully parked like the forgotten fragment of a sentence. Mailboxes forged into functional art also make the list, along with forgotten tractors overgrown in blackberries, and old barns whistling in the wind. All project a sense of wonder as I pass because they are still charged with that magic where every soul believed in the promise of a brighter future.

Loggers horse pull monument in Bend

Old Hudson near Amity

Rusty mine equipment

Victorian era doorknobs at Hippo Hardware

1912 steam tractor at Wooden Shoe tulips

1912 Farm machinery

Model T in Bend

Railroad bench

Old working class pull taps in Carlton

Tools at the Aurora Museum

SNOHOMISH
WESTERN AUTO
ASSOCIATE STORE
Mobilgas
SOCONY-VACUUM

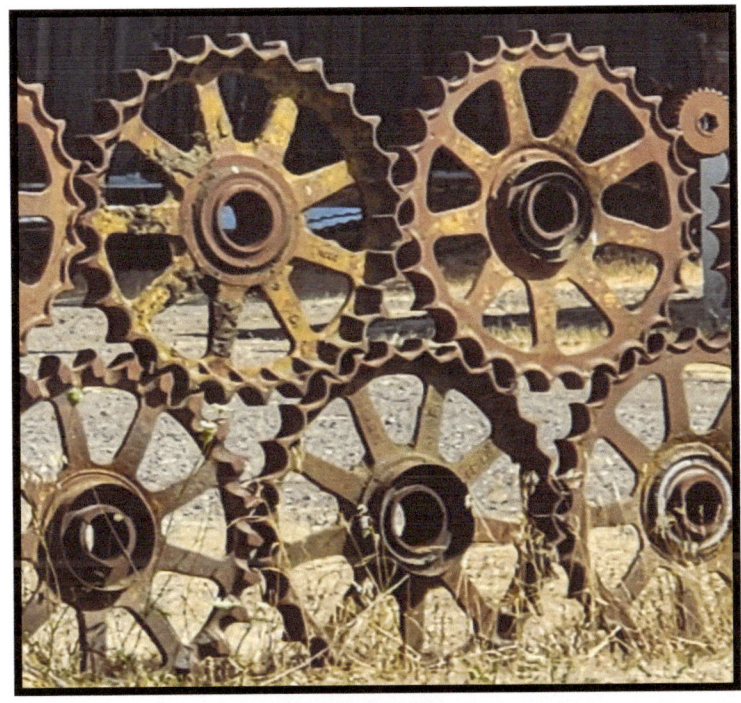

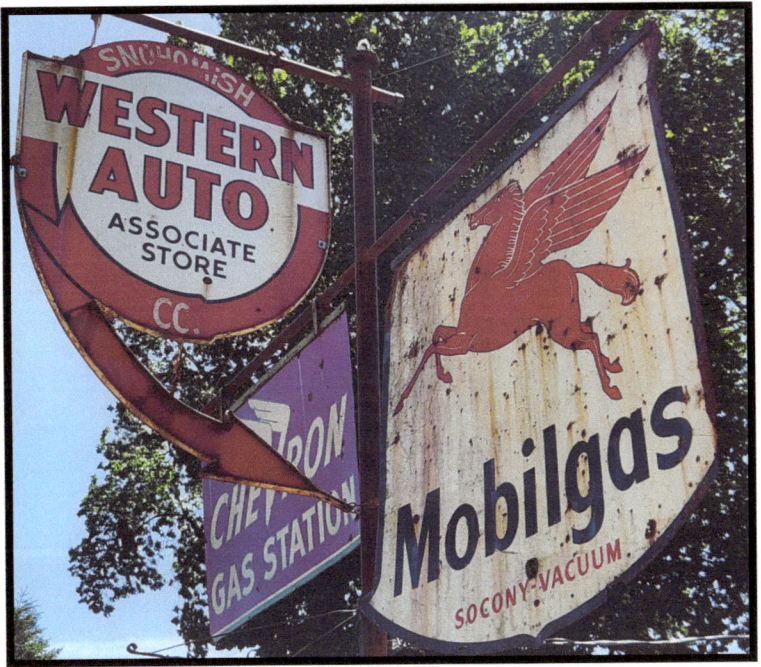

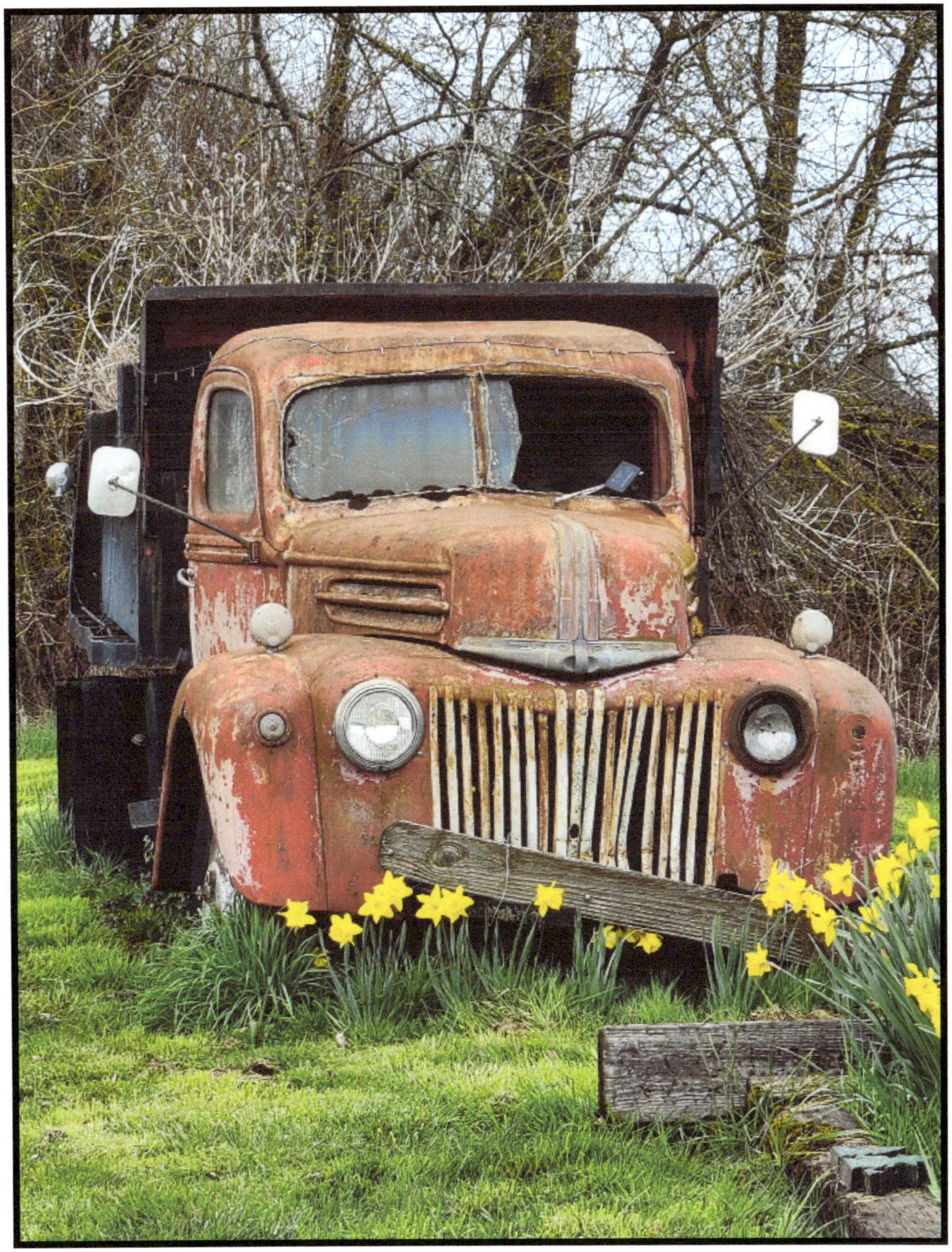

Happy Trails

As a native Oregonian, you might not appreciate the enormity of the task contained within picking out trails of interest after fifty years of poking around much of the state's forests. Oregon is a place filled with varied environments offering not only beautiful views, but intense natural experiences that influence emotions while recharging spirit. Commit part of your day to driving and suddenly you possess an ability to visit high desert, juniper forest, multiple riparian zones, waterfalls, lava covered mountains, and hidden, misty rain forest. Every zone has its appeal, altered by the time of day or severity of season; a site at winter dusk can be completely different from a summer morning. Baskett Slough National Wildlife Refuge has underscored this effect for me. A lucky find some thirty years ago, this bird sanctuary outside Portland provided a closeness that allowed me to experience every combination of weather and sun. With luck, a visitor in late spring will find Dusky Geese gathered on the west hill set off by a hair trigger. They will erupt in flight with the slightest provocation from a Bald Eagle. If conditions are right, they circle overhead, nervously honking and flapping before sinking into formation like a noisy, eclectic bomber fleet.

The combination of birds to my experience can change daily. From the same parking spot, on a little patch of gravel, I've watched hundreds of barn swallows dive and turn like fighter jets, gulping down emerging mosquitos, only to find Northern Shovelers and Pintails floating the following day. There is an odd casting call that rotates geese, to shore birds, to low level hunters. Oregon has a peculiar quality, a quality I've rarely experienced outside the state, what I've come to know as "subtle intensity." A characteristic that seems to match the personality of those born here with the environments they inhabit.

Tamolitch Falls Blue Pool trail

Fall includes subtle browns and yellows, unlike the vibrant oranges of the Northeast, and water that bubbles over boulders at a leisurely pace often whispering soft poetry amidst a crashing rage. Even the deep blue Pacific, with its legions of invading waves and fierce undertow, has a quieter side. I often find myself in the soothing breeze, sitting near swaying pale grasses, writing in my journal. The azure blue blurs into a softer green by shore as teal topped waves stretch far inland, teasing your toes. I have found myself on many occasions subconsciously singing ancient sea shanties unknown to recorded history, but somehow find a new home passing from my lips.

Long walks in Oregon are not about getting there. Rather, they are about exploring a moment. Finding yourself lost on a trail is no time for unfolding maps or exchanging business cards. I think back on a late summer evening with my best friend Kris in Pacific City. He has inherited the family cabin in recent years and much to his credit, became familiar with the rhythm of the sea and the salmon.

One evening while visiting, we chose to climb the sand wall at the north end of the beach. A place I had tumbled as a child, testing my limits while sowing a growing love for the water and stone of the left coast. This particular evening, Kris and I topped the steep hill out of breath, hands on knees before emptying our sand filled shoes. The sky was painted in classic orange, as the sun put on a fireworks show rarely equaled in life, prompting Kris and I to sit silently, lost in the sunset. After a few minutes, two families totaling eight people puffed their way over the rim of the ascent. We watched with interest as the children wrestled each other hyped up by the climb. The four adults gazed toward the horizon a few moments...

I turned to Kris giggling, completely baffled at how anyone could do anything but drop their everything for ten minutes to bask in the spectacular show unfolding before them. Oregon will offer you many such opportunities, but it is your job to pay attention and receive them. So, I've developed some trail rules for viewing sunsets or hiking trails in the state based on five decades of experience. One, consider going another time if you are not fully prepared to commit to being there. I remember visiting a national park some years ago and felt a bit discouraged when I found a full parking lot. I needn't have worried though, as once the majority got their selfie near the main attraction (usually within a couple hundred feet), most feebly returned to their car without interacting with the landscape. Two, slow down and breathe. Nature isn't a race or a competition. If you are going to really see a stretch of untouched earth with eyes of wonder that the cosmos had intended, open yourself to it, stop looking at your watch. Three, enough of the gadgets already. To immerse yourself in landscape, put the cell phone on silent mode and slide it into your back pocket. I love taking pictures but getting into a groove only nature can provide, involves being present; not dragging around 10 pounds of equipment for setting up graduation photos under a pine tree. When you see something truly spectacular, especially during your first visit, get the shot on your cell, put it away, and keep moving. Four, be quiet. I cannot tell you how many times I've heard families yelling at each other a half mile away before seeing them. Focus so as to avoid becoming one of these Neanderthals. Training your kids to be quiet and respectful in nature will give them an early start on appreciation and other hikers will be grateful. We need that appreciation if we are going to keep some of these sites alive for future generations.

As noted, I've hiked my share of trails and natural areas. I'll include a few favorites below, but since I experienced a powerful first-time hike in Bend recently, I'd like to run through my visit there, and how I approach a new landscape. The Riley Natural area is five miles or so north of the city. I was pleasantly surprised by the length and the beauty of the site as the parking lot was filled with social seniors who didn't appear to be winded. I maintained a positive attitude, saying a few hellos before looking over the site map, and taking three deep breaths at the trail head. The lower canyon loop appeared the best option as it was the furthest from the general crowd. I love isolation in wilderness and never allow fear of wild animals to keep me from a beautiful spot. Instead, I run through my best options if I do have an encounter (black bear or cougar), and how I should respond. This primarily involves actively staying alert. Fully present means I don't have *Rage Against the Machine* blasting in my earbuds as I walk a trail.

The first few hundred yards I observed some juniper trees surrounding a high sage plain with a spectacular view of the misty Cascade Range in the distance. It appeared the majority of the hikers were completing the first loop, choosing to stick to the plain before turning back. The air was beginning to heat up, so I knew I would need to track my energy level as I often choose to walk light rather than bring a metal water container. I always hydrate just before hiking as my way to cheat that extra weight. It was only a couple hundred yards in when I arrived at a series of hairpin turns that descended to the floor of the small valley where large, heavy stones were used as steps to reinforce the heavily used trail. Two minutes in and I peered back to see all sorts of jumbled basalts lining the incline. I took out my cell phone to play with composition as it's just such spots that make great guides for watercolors.

Just then an exhausted jogger, shirt off, huffing, ran by me never looking up. I suppose he might have lived a few miles away, but such sunny, cool days are few in this part of the world and must be soaked in. I took a deep breath before descending the trail loops, enjoying the fresh Ponderosa pine. I then controlled my breath for a quick meditation.

Alaskan cedar raised trail

Pressing a hand against an old grown tree, I spoke a short blessing, thanking the wilderness for such peace and quiet. I continued my stroll, looking side-to-side, determined to enjoy every step my feet press into the ground. Spontaneously, I broke into a few bars of song. No idea as to the origins of my lyrics, though I am open to letting the land influence my mind. I slowed down, enjoying every side view, until hearing the bubbling of water nearby. I smelled a small stream running through the valley earlier, but this was the first point I made contact on the trail. I headed directly for the noise, immediately feeling cool air from a soft wind. I found a clear break in the forest canopy, so I skipped from patch to patch across the rust-colored duff to avoid stomping the small saplings. An important element of the natural experience for me is leaving everything as I've found it. Nothing ruins the experience like the occasional beer can or AA batteries tossed in some shrubs.

The stream was a deep olive-green, slowly meandering around basaltic boulders. The rolling water was meditative, luring me into a hypnotic state as I admired the gentle water through a tangle of thick brush. I took three deep breaths and raised my hands skyward to remain fully present. Out loud, I said a prayer asking whoever was listening to forgive the intrusion and continue blessing this place. I then backtrack my way out along the same path, walking more slowly this time, accessing my heightened awareness to just observe. The boulder size seemed to be increasing as I passed one behemoth dislodged from the cliffs above. I placed my hands upon its surface, then closed my eyes. I always feel an ancient energy in such stones. Even with the cool surface, that history of lava fire lay tucked away deep within. Soon the volume of the water increased, and I skipped along a path of stone reaching toward the water. The sun was warm now, but the stream cold and alive. I closed my eyes, breathing deeply, so as

to commit it to memory. It helps me in times of stress to revisit such places as they often recharge me. I moved on and began to look more closely at the vegetation, before a small marten, bouncing along the lip of shore, spotted me. He stopped, raised his head, and looked me over curiously. I've learned from my time in wilderness that animals often reflect your state of emotion, so I was careful to remain calm, and avoid disrupting his routine. I spoke to him softly.

"Hello little one, you have nothing to worry about, I'm not going to hurt you."

He paused before bouncing toward the river where he smoothly slid to the center of a thick bush curling at its center. I spoke again. This unexpected creature finally got the best of him as he lifted his head, unwrapping his body. Cautiously, he wormed his long black body out of his fort of branches to take a good look, seeking to assess the danger from this kind stranger. It appeared few humans responded positively upon seeing this small, fury animal. Most I am sure, succumbed to fear.

Years before, my best friend and I were sitting in a small park at the edge of town. We were calmly chatting when screams rose from several adults watching their children at the playground Island. They spotted a pair of young bucks nervously prancing across the street heading right for us. An older couple walking their dog paused in terror pointing at the duo as they approached us on the grass. I recall breathing deeply, carefully maintaining a peaceful state as the two trotted past panting. We watched them unconcerned, hoping the outbursts wouldn't spook them into becoming aggressive. It didn't, and they melted into a wall of shrubs at the boundary of the park.

My little fellow soon bounced off down the riverbank as well, leaving me with a strange feeling of connection and isolation in the same moment. Perhaps the connection comes from my ancestors who spent thousands of years wandering such places. They would have been equally enveloped by it, seeing terror and the joy in the natural rhythms of life. I feel that flow of the past through my blood into the present. Radiating a beautiful universal consciousness free from time. The hum of life everywhere. Perhaps my feelings of isolation come from the realization that I am twenty minutes from the safety and luxuries to which we have grown so accustomed. While I don't object to a good massage or glass of wine, I do feel we've become chained to our habits. We are often blind to experiences of real freedom found in the waves or meadow flowers as the natural gift of place, and that power of place is invigorating.

I continued on, noticing the dark basaltic rocks began to increasing in size and frequency. The water worked harder now, gaining speed, roaring as it passed. I admired an angular cliff of yellow and brown ten feet above the water line swirling green. There exist spots in the world where the land is so quiet you can hear the sound of blood flowing through your ears between heartbeats. I was completely absorbed when a high-pitched squeal broke the air. I realized I was about to encounter my second group of humans since entering the canyon. Perhaps I would curl up at the center of a shrub.

There was a quick rise in the path before it descended into a bowl of stone surrounding flat earth where a family of five sat drinking coke along the stream side. Open backpacks were scattered everywhere spilling packaged foods. They seemed nice enough, smiling as I passed, but I couldn't help seeing them as the animals do; self-absorbed. Empties were scattered around mom's feet as children yelled over each other while hopping from boulder to boulder in colorful clothing. Dad was waist deep in the water, content sipping his beer while splashing the kids around him. I moved on. The final phase required I puff up the previous switchbacks until finding the bluish-green sage again.

It is routine for me to take notes upon my return to the car, writing in a small booklet removed from my backpack. I star those entries I wish to remember, and one day return to. Interesting sites and favorites will develop their own history each time I pass. Some evolve into meditation spots while others provide a grueling workout with the reward of a breathtaking view. Avoid the mistake of separating yourself from the environment with a massive investment in equipment or tech. A nature spot is filled with vibrant energy, unconcerned with programing a fish finder or creating a layered Gucci look. Perhaps it is the only place you are allowed to be real.

Driving

Driving Oregon outside the high traffic density of Portland is one of the more peace-inducing hobbies I've picked up in the state. I'm a native of course, so I like to think I'm a bit more immune to the culture of hurry,

"Don't be late! You have an appointment! Eat fast, we're leaving!"

I did have one gigantic advantage to counterbalance the blasphemous cult of running though: my father. He was an elementary school principal who grew up in a large family when traditional values still ruled the household. Mom reminded me over dinner that even though he had the savings to buy a new car whenever he wanted, he never got around to owning one. I never saw him drive across town where he didn't take his time enjoying his surroundings, or ever choose to wear a tie outside of a board meeting. Perhaps wrestling with a bout of polio early in his second year of college, ending a promising future in athletics, gave him insight as to the true value of living and a greater appreciation for those things he had; his family, his education, his sense of humor. The experience did leave him with one weakened arm but never dampened the spirit of the tri-athlete, football playing lover of life he'd developed into from childhood. His home in Eastern Oregon was stuffed with brothers and sisters, perhaps accounting for his role as the pragmatist, a quality that influenced how he made his choice of college at the end of high school.

After winning their divisional football championship in the fifties, his best friend Bill West, shared the story of how the two selected the site of their college attendance. We were standing around wasting time during the halftime break at the boys' high school state basketball championship some forty years ago when he told the tale. Apparently, both he and my father were offered scholarships to the University of Oregon and Oregon State University, with no particular loyalty to either school. They put off making a final decision until the end of the summer with only a limited time remaining to commit one way or the other. Both packed and slung one bag over their shoulders before walking to route 84 at the edge of town. They hitchhiked side-by-side for two long hours until both became frustrated. A decision was made to split up taking opposite sides of the freeway to see if one large dope was more appealing that two large dopes. Bill was the first to attract a ride as someone pulled over ten minutes later. The gentleman said he was heading to Corvallis through Portland, and so Bill called over to dad,

"Looks like Oregon State pal, see you later!' then hopped in the passenger seat and was gone.

My father began walking, feeling a bit depressed, knowing his friend was on his way to college while he stood stagnant. Suddenly, another car pulled over, this time heading to Eugene by way of Bend; so it was he would be a duck. The story remains a favorite brewpub tale among friends, and I like to think it's because it captures the country innocence of the time, and a willingness to trust your future on the toss of a coin.

Outside of a solo beer on Friday nights, my father's single greatest indulgence was the slow cruise he'd take around town each evening observing the changes that had passed while working at his desk. I learned the value of slowing things down with a good drive from him. To this day, I rarely go five over the speed limit just in case I happen upon some untraveled wood, or peculiar piece of architecture. The slow drag, as I call it, has become a big exercise in remaining present.

Brachiosaur

When investigating a popular spot, it is best to plan a satisfying road trip apart from the cramped sites of Labor Day or traffic before and after Thanksgiving. What a pity to have one's natural ruminations interrupted by angry drivers screaming for velocity. For me, it's the call of wilderness and farmland that has bewitched my soul to wander, a will to explore that road less traveled because I must know what lay beyond that wheat covered hill. Oregon has plenty of both, a multitude of landscapes and flora possessing the variety of a college era mixtape. There are sweet country ballads, thumping metal solos, and unforgettable pop classics that lead one to dance and whirl among swaying pines in time with the passing clouds.

A trip on I-84 from Ontario to Pendleton allows me to enter a daydream state, pondering relatives who fought incredible odds settling this wild land. Wallowa Lake was a favorite swimming hole for grandmother and mom and is where famed Nez Pierce Chief Joseph was buried on an overlooking hill. Blistering hot in summer, unbearably cold in winter, there's still magic to this land. The raw bursting energy of creation still fills the young volcanic rock with sparking vibration. The crumbling seams are filled with mystic old growth and angular quartz gems. An easy place to find peace as the shadows of an ancient wood provides another form of freedom. A place beyond leaf blowers and tax filings.

Ankylosaurus

As I-84 continues, the run from The Dalles to Portland is one of the best drives in the West as far as I'm concerned. With recent fire damage, the U-shaped blocky cliffs echo that fierce wall of water that tumbled down the Columbia to create the Columbia Gorge 10,000 years ago. I rarely make recommendations about the Gorge, as I do not wish to deprive the curious hiker from making their own discoveries as Lewis and Clark had done while drifting down this beautiful watercourse.

I've been to many beaches around the world, but the long stretches of public accessible sand in Oregon remain my favorite. We have Governor Tom McCall ('67 to '75) to thank for that. He was a white-haired cantankerous conservative who saw the trend to privatize our coastline and pushed the Oregon Beaches Bill to ensure all citizens retained access. He received national attention for saying,

"Come again and again. But for heaven's sake, don't move here to live. Or if you do have to move in to live, don't tell any of your neighbors where you are going." (1971)

I thank him every time I walk along the tidal zone listening to the roar of the waves. U.S. Coastal Highway 101 begins in Astoria and follows the very rugged, rocky coastline prone to slumps and sinkholes all the way to the California Redwoods. Thirty miles off the coast sits the subduction zone for the Juan de Fuca plate where it squeezes its way under the much larger North American plate. This has wreaked havoc to the region in the past of course, but it mostly remains hidden within the vast scope of geologic time. The Mount St. Helens eruption of 1980 was a powerful reminder for how tenuous our hold on the land may be, and every Oregonian accepts the risk of tragedy as the price for living within such expansive beauty.

As a dinosaur kid, I must confess I loved the 101 as it passed the Prehistoric Gardens south of Port Orford. I'd regularly spout off facts about triceratops or stegosaurus from the posters that covered my walls. To this day, I still get giddy when the ticket staff tell me that feeding the exhibits is forbidden and dangerous. I am in love with random kitsch, and during my last visit, I discussed this obsession with a pair of retired women visiting from Michigan. We'd been openly ooOOOoo-ing over the spiny ankylosaur walking into a bank of leafy, green ferns when we faced off. Dinosaur talk easily leads to a discussion of the legendary Pixie Kitchen in Lincoln City; a local kitsch Mecca for those who enjoyed seeing pixies riding spouting whales, or playing early versions of video games in the basement. It was the first time I'd ever seen a wheat thin or tried a hush puppy. Old Lincoln City used to have go carts and taffy, and restaurants strewn with heavy fishing nets holding Japanese floats.

As an adult, I spent ten years traveling the coast exploring the various Bed and Breakfasts. A memorable stay was at Sylvia Beach Hotel (a very B and B feel) in Newport where rooms have a theme. We stayed in the corner F. Scott Fitzgerald room, enjoying a slice of beach with the street view below. I was intrigued by the Edgar Allen Poe room next door and planned to stay there on our next visit, but the red-eyed raven perched above started giving me a creepy feeling, so, I've yet to follow through. The downstairs dinner was communal and came with an added bonus. Guests were instructed to play a game as a table, which turned out to be a great ice breaker as we shared much more openly with other guests. I think any kind of personal touch extends your enjoyment, as most tend to never leave their room.

Down the road, we took a day trip to Newport. After making several trips to the Oregon Aquarium in grade school, with teacher's index fingers planted firmly in my back for not following rules, I finally made it to the Hatfield Marine Science Visitor Center just up the road. The place is filled with hands-on displays, local history, science, and cultural exhibits. Initially, the center gives an appearance of a children's museum, as young ones bounce and squeal, running from case to case, as mom and dad try to keep up. There is a wonderful sea life touching area where you can feel sea anemones grip your fingers with tentacles. What appears to be an old leather shoe at first, is in fact a beautiful sea slug. For me, the real attraction is the small fee which allows such a great mix of different children to explore with wonder. It is an inspirational and powerful reminder about the spectacular world we live in.

Variations for travel off the 101 are endless. You may turn off Hwy 26 from Portland to shortcut down Hwy 53. I love perusing the coastal farm country in the Fall within the rich riparian zone, exploding with color reflecting off the river in October. A quick turn off 53 will bring you to Soapstone Lake, a well-worn, but doable nature trail with old growth and water views. I love returning in the winter when I can have the site to myself. There is a full pantheon of birds to listen to, content in their isolation. After rejoining Highway 101 at Nehalem, stop for soup at Buttercups Ice Creams and Chowders before looking through the shops. A neighbor gifted me a quart some months ago, and though a bit spendy, you will be hooked. Follow the narrow sidewalk behind Buttercups to find Riverside Fish and Chips, where I love to watch paddle boarders head down a side branch of the Nehalem River as Barn Swallows gather mud for nest building in the spring.

Dino building Monmouth

Variations for travel off the 101 are endless. You may turn off Hwy 26 from Portland to shortcut down Hwy 53. I love perusing the coastal farm country in the Fall within the rich riparian zone exploding with color reflecting off the river in October. A quick turn off 53 will bring you to Soapstone Lake, a well-worn, but doable nature trail with old growth and water views. I love returning in the winter when I can have the site to myself. There is a full pantheon of birds to listen to, content in their isolation. After rejoining Highway 101 at Nehalem, stop for soup at Buttercups Ice Creams and Chowders before looking through the shops. A neighbor gifted me a quart some months ago, and though a bit spendy, you will be hooked. Follow the narrow sidewalk leading behind Buttercups to

Haystack Rock also known as Chief Kiawanda Rock

find Riverside Fish and Chips, where I love to watch paddle boarders head down a side branch of the Nehalem River as Barn Swallows gather mud for nest building in the spring.

Keep following 101 south to enjoy an easy slide through Wheeler and Rockaway Beach, making sure to stop at The Rockaway Big Tree Trailhead to visit the most amazing Alaskan Yellow Cedar. Maybe you'll see faces and shapes as I do in the old, wrinkled bark. Continue on and just before Garibaldi you'll pass what I call the Japanese Islands. In town, if you make a right turn to the shoreline, you'll find a rundown shack of a place that used to be The Garibaldi Cannery. I shared my love of catfish with a Southerner there who told me Oregonians would never get it. The shop used to send out a troller every morning to sell whatever they caught and sell it in a glass display case inside. On lucky days, you'd find halibut. We'd have it bagged up with ice and drive like mad to have get it in the oven as soon as possible. The fish was so fresh, it felt like eating a stick of butter. While gone, the nearby Captains Corners Seafood Market will give visitors a similar experience without the small, peeling shack.

Traveling down Hwy 99 through McMinnville and Otis is another interesting access point to the coast. When you get to the Y branching left to Lincoln City or right to Pacific City, take the right ramp first to find a small United Nations protected coastal environment. It's an immediate left, just after the right. I always appreciate visiting a place similar to the way Native Americans saw it. If you continue north for a short drive, turn west on Brooten Road to enter the small town of Pacific City. Cross the bridge near the center of town that appears to end in sand dunes. Then take the immediate left until you reach the Bob Straub State Park parking area. It's one of my favorite little parks in the world. Outside the summer season, you will often find yourself alone walking near powerful aqua waves as they chase small Sanderlings up the sand. Small groups of pelicans often fly just offshore as you enjoy the view of Haystack Rock (2), also known as Chief Kiawanda Rock. I must confess, I'm mystified by the tale the tracks left by visitors tell. They often appear as a funnel path leading to the surf line before turning back to return to the bank. I followed the churned-up sand during one visit and ended up by an elderly couple. My answer came when they raised a selfie stick, forced a smile, then returned to their car. I will never understand visiting a place just to brag about visiting it when there is so much to soak in and enjoy. I could sit there all day just listening to the power and rhythm of the waves. It's one of the few places I break out in random poetry as I walk. Up the road a few spots remain to park at the Blue Pelican Brewpub. There is a traditional Oregonian climb up the sand wall there just beyond the crowd at the boundary of Kiwanda State Natural Area. It remains one of my favorite spots to view a sunset in the country. This is not a moment to rush. Dinner can wait, sit down and experience the view. Afterward, I love to travel a little further North to drive down Sand Lake Road. There is a beautiful hillside view of the bay where I took a photographer friend last fall. A beautiful transparent fog hung over the hills creating artistic silhouettes of the fishermen casting their lines.

For the times I continue south from Garibaldi on 101, I enter the community of Tillamook. It still clings to that small town charm I grew up in, but I think it well represents the ongoing tug-o-war taking place between traditional businesses and a stream of trendy new arrivals. Cities like McMinnville have seen a flood of out-of-state businesses replacing smaller, long-established ones. I grew up within the wine tasting culture and enjoy many local pinots, but when the trickle became a flood, the downtown was vastly changed by tasting rooms at the expense of community feelings.

Monkey Puzzle Trees

As I passed Tillamook this day, I wanted to sample a brewpub that had received some enthusiastic write-ups in local press. It seemed to be a new kind of concept pub that created "inoculated" beer products producing interesting, praiseworthy flavors. I'm very curious about cutting edge newcomers and do my best on a first visit to keep an open mind while retaining a critical eye. Barley got the first tour as we stopped for photos near some of the large barrels placed around the exterior of the building. The staff were eager and friendly, clearly passionate

Monkey's greenhouse

about the product they pitched for the de Garde brewpub. Over two trips I managed to try the fruity pinot favorite, Archer, and the more IPA-like Ivy beer favorite. The drinks and the company were a wonderful break from the lengthy drive home, but there is something in the streamlined atmosphere I continue to struggle with. I recalled a conversation with a millennial who referred to her idea of elegance as "a minimal, curated style." This seemed to hit the nail on the head because my idea of elegance takes a backseat, baby boomer that I am, to a warm social climate. I remain hopeful that as modern businesses become absorbed by the surrounding culture, they will see the value of adding plants, photos, and local products, before hosting community events that welcome a broader spectrum of fans. I stay optimistic..

Continuing south, I accidentally happened upon another business that was literally Oregon grown. In the middle of the swift, rising turn just beyond the Hudson House Inn, sat a sandwich board message, Monkey Puzzle Trees for Sale. Caught in a whim I spun up the short, meandering gravel road before finding myself parked near a small home. Instantly, I was circled by a happy, energetic puppy before a slightly gray, smiling woman emerged from a side door.

"The folks at the nursery in town call me Monkey," she said, "welcome!" Not the usual greeting to which I'm accustomed, so I became intrigued.

I believe Monkey told me her real name was Barbara, though I'm not sure. What I did know, was I grew up with a Monkey Puzzle tree in front of the town library, a point I explained to Monkey before I was treated to the full tour. We strolled around the house until reaching the Monkey tree nursery. There, each young sprout, looking like a Ponderosa Pine pinecone scale, was placed in a small cup in rows of 15 to 20. She explained these young seedlings were like the chocolate covered caramels of the animal world. If she didn't have them carefully screened in and nailed securely, every chipmunk, squirrel, jay, and raccoon for a mile would feast off them until gorged. Further along behind the house were the larger potted adults ranging in size from ten inches to three feet.

"I won't sell them until they reach three feet!" she said, "any shorter, and people who don't know how to properly take care of these guys come back holding a dead tree."

As I looked over the range of sizes my curiosity got the best of me. "So why the passion over the Monkey Puzzle trees? Why not Tibetan Spruce, or Australian Pine?" The question seemed well worn as she looked up a bit sad.

"They're from Chile and endangered," she answered, putting on her gloves. "They are one of the most unusual trees I've ever come across and I just can't stand the thought of their exit from the earth." I nodded and asked if I could look around a bit more. She smiled and immediately started mixing a large batch of fertilizer.

I was only there for ten minutes when I felt completely at ease. The two small, enclosed greenhouses were filled with flowering plants along with other interesting exotics. I had to remind myself that it was still January! There was a hominess to the place as well as something more intangible. An indescribable realness to her purpose and the loving care she put towards her tasks. I'd felt this before, visiting my best friend's green house in Carlton, where beyond reason, he'd created a citrus grove Eden in the cold shadow of the Coastal Range. It's just this feeling of connection that can never be expressed fully through an artboard design. A light fueled by a selfless devotion to service and love. I leave Monkey with a promise to return.

There are so many little such adventures across the state, too many to name, but to finish my coastal tour, I'll mention a few other favorite stops. I love the Air Museum on the south end of Tillamook, not for the planes, but for the massive wood housing that once held a large observation blimp during World War 2. Occasionally I honor my father's love for fresh oysters with a stop at Jandy's, then gather a bouquet at Old House Dahlias up the road for mom. I've become fond of another brief stop in Neskowin, just off the highway, where the "ghost trees" can now be seen across the small stream dividing the beach. An old growth forest buried in a large slump 2,000 years ago has now been uncovered by waves.

In Lincoln City I can't get enough of the Otis Café before wandering around the elbow at Taft Waterfront Park. I've always been attracted to spots where powerful watercourses meet, and this is where the Siletz River wrestles for dominance with the incoming tide as sea lions lazily sun themselves on the opposing shore. Touring the glass blowing shops is a newer hobby in town. Twice in my life I've managed to take the tour from Depot Bay to watch the California Gray Whale migration north. There are no words to capture the emotion I feel when blessed to be so close to these beautiful animals. Heading south, I gain a new respect for the Yaquina Bay bridge in Newport every time I cross, and while I've only visited the dunes in Florence once as a college student,

Geology

My wife is originally from Massachusetts, but her eyes were set on Oregon long before we met. We'd both been geology geeks as kids, always picking up and collecting unusual stones, and we even owned the same blue handled field pick. When I returned home soon after meeting her at an Arizona archaeological field project, we signed on with an old, crotchety professor to walk the Blue Mountains searching for Native cultural remains. I celebrated my 30th birthday in that country, driving to

Rice Museum Crystal display

Heppner for the most welcome shower of my life followed by a second rate, glorious pizza. Rocks became a binding theme in our life together. My wife developed an interest in jewelry and took a variety of smithing classes while collecting a shelfs worth of high-grade tools. Soon, many of our holidays/birthdays meant adventurous agate hunts along the banks of rivers. My path through Oregon geology developed earlier in life with a fascination for fossils (especially trilobites), cementing a lifelong interest after Norm Combs, local grocer, led our fourth-grade class to a railroad trestle outside Vernonia. It was here in a bank of mudstone, near the railroad, that shells and small fish were preserved. Norm's son Brian, a good friend and classmate, always spent summers at Camp Hancock (sponsored by the Oregon Museum of Science and Industry) near the

Trilobite

Schist in light

Rock show

Crystals at Rice Museum

John Day fossil hunting site. When he returned, he'd always let me examine items from the camp a few weeks before school started. My wife and I have grown particularly fond of the green schist from the Illinois River Valley where the road follows along beside some of the most ancient stone in the state. With the sun blazing overhead, the quartz in the stone glimmers like diamonds while locals speed by.

Willamette River

In the summer after the spring floods recede, we often search the banks of the Willamette River between Salem and Newberg for agates. A recent trip along the Nehalem River outside of Nehalem proper, found us looking for Carnelian agate in the shallow pools just off Hwy 26. We've come to recognize geology crowds by their hunched over side-to-side swaying at places like Fogerty beach, in their hunt for treasure. As a child, I was fond of visiting Agate Beach, which has become lost to us now geologically due to weather changes. I loved the rich golden color as you held up a stone in the setting sun. I'd collect all of my findings into an old Hills Brothers' coffee can I stored at the back of my closet like pirates' treasure. Only to be shared with trusted friends.

In recent years, I found this can at the bottom of a box of old winter sweaters, long absent from the glory of the sun. Because there are so many that hoard in this hobby, I decided it just wasn't fair to deprive other young children the thrill of finding such agates for themselves while strolling a long stretch of beach, lost in a daydream. Even after a big storm, it is rare to find a stone larger than a pea these days, so I took them back to an isolated section of beach for release. Let them be magic in the eyes of another child, rather than a dusty trophy for a middle-aged man. As our children become more interested in watching YouTube videos or playing cell phone games, I feel we owe them some magic in this world. Something discovered unexpectedly.

Cafes & Coffee Shops

I'd walked into a popular coffee shop chain a few months after covid was in its first decline hoping for a moment of normal tedium when I made a discovery. The shop had received a complete face lift, not only changing the artwork and tables, but the number of seats dropped from 26 to 12 available chairs. I must admit to being a bit upset by that changes as what I find best and most nourishing concerning coffee shops or small cafés is the intimacy they bring to our world of rushing without the need for efficiency. An ability exists within their walls to just sit and read for an hour, purchase local honey, or laugh at two brothers wrestling over control of a beat-up couch. And those that are truly community based, hold people discussing their passions, negotiating business pricing, or just sit grinning with a deeply held appreciation for life. Once these places become overly sanitized, covid, or no covid, they will become just another caffeine line as good as the next and we've all lost something.

Urban Grange

While many post-covid coffee shops have appeared to lose their mojo this way, there still exists a rare few with that vibration of life and authenticity that still make it worth the trip. I have found there are several components to a great coffee shop.

One, a great coffee shop is usually on the fringe. *Urban Grange* in West Salem fits this description in a number of ways. I once walked in and snapped a quick photo of the entire shop so I could practice sketching background crowds for an upcoming graphic novel, when some guy slapped a note down hard at my table before storming out in a huff. It read, taking photos is a bad idea and never include me in the future. Now that's the kind of coffee shop spunk that gets you on this list. The customer profile changes pretty much daily, so, you may find yourself near a seed church

Ike Box

Stumptown Coffee Roasters

pastor trying to sell a hipper version of Jesus to teenagers one day, only to find seniors playing score four with their grandkids at the same table the next. That's community.

Two, a great coffee shop is often quirky with an undeniable personality. *Ike Box* near Downtown Salem has this vibe, though the staff are too on top of things to give that lazy, what day is this expression so universal in chill places. I love their hip quotes of the day posted on a roll of brown packaging paper bolted to the wall behind the ordering line. The place leans toward hipness, but I still love the occasional random person who goes off on the inexplicable rant about deer antlers or a lost sock or something without warning. I suspect many are homeless hoisting a

The Black Ink in Oregon City

celebratory black coffee after turning in a towering mass of bottle deposits. Another dimension to the charm. The real star for me is the interior, which appears to be some kind of 19th century realist interpretation of an opera house. I have never inquired as to its background, or the classic design with raised stage, romantic painted backdrops, and squared support columns hinting at some storied past. Another old favorite recently returned to my radar as the result of a wrong turn onto Belmont in Portland. *Stumptown Coffee Roasters* has an almost seventies punk feel to it when you walk in, the barista in thick black eyeliner and an array of metal spikes on her wrists. It was the strange deck of cards sporting oddballs and bodybuilders under the shop name that instantly stood out, along with a very powerful brick wall in the bathroom covered with graffiti. It is such locations that stir powerful daydreams that lead to interesting stories.

Three, a great coffee shop always has interesting things to look at as you wait for your order. Message boards, political essays, and event posters may play a part, but books or trinkets are a particular favorite to occupy the mind. I happened to read about *The Black Ink* in Oregon City a week before running an errand there, so my trip luckily aligned with a stop in. The establishment was on high covid alert at the time, but they still managed to serve one of the spiciest Chai Teas I've ever had. Shelves of books are always a winner with me, but it was the Sasquatch gear and mugs that won me over as a first-time visitor. I look forward to visiting when things resemble something close to normal again, so I can chat with regulars.

Stimulus Pacific City

Haystack Rock

Powell's Books on Burnside also fits the category. It provides a level of people watching, ranking up there with Las Vegas, without the alcohol. Nothing quite like sipping tea in a chill environment after grabbing a stack of books off the nearby graphic novel section! What could I possibly say to express my gratitude for the many acres of thought Powell's has provided me through the years? If aliens landed on the waterfront of West Portland tomorrow for a tour, I'd probably take them to Powell's. The place gives me that big city fix when it's been a long winter. Every individual is so absorbed by their reading they rarely make eye contact or even consider disturbing you. An odd mix of crowding with peace, somewhat like the Tokyo subway system.

Four, a great coffee shop has something you can get nowhere else. When I passed through Pacific City on a coastal rain afternoon with my best friend

Kris, he asked if I'd ever been to a trendy little place called, *Stimulus*. A boxy coffee shop bakery coyly placed across the street from the Blue Heron brew pub, right on the beach. I hadn't, so we quickly spun into a side street. The interior was nothing to write home about, but the baked goods made me skip right over the mugs and beans to the counter. Kris recommended the savory sweet Beach Bun, and before long, I was wearing it on my lap and coat. The bun was noteworthy enough, but once I turned around, I fully realized the appeal of the location. Through the rain-soaked windows I could see the towering presence of Haystack Rock almost a mile off the shoreline. There is always peace in a great view.

Finally, a great coffee shop has great coffee. When I first read about Aussie owned *Proud Mary*, the reviews raved it was the best coffee in the city, so of course, I showed up within the week.

Proud Mary

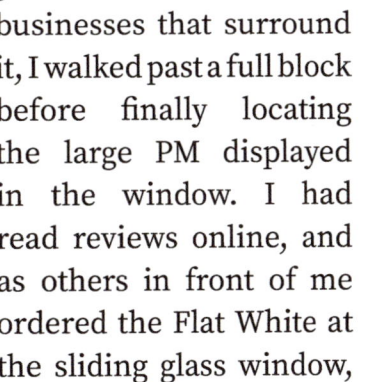

The shop is so effectively camouflaged in the row of small businesses that surround it, I walked past a full block before finally locating the large PM displayed in the window. I had read reviews online, and as others in front of me ordered the Flat White at the sliding glass window, I decided to plunge right in and try one for myself. Honestly, I had not drunk straight up coffee in two years as hypertension had been targeted by my doctor. The Flat White, it turns out, was a cup of espresso with steamed milk that not only went down quickly and smooth but packed quite a punch. The eight ounces had me flying for two hours after I finished. I understood once again why coffee had become so popular in America.

Reading at the Coffee Cat

Mom at the Crescent

Breakfast sandwich at Red Hills Deli in Dundee

Fresh ocean halibut from Garibaldi

EZ Orchards

*HALF order of Don's Mess
at White's Restaurant*

Dear Old Friend

If there were ever an old cliché that applied equally to 1940 as it does today, it would be my feelings toward the furry by-product of wolves currently known as, man's best friend. The Soft-Coated Wheaten Terrier, Irish cat poop eating, deer carcass rolling, stubborn Billy goat Tom Sawyer dog currently in my possession that frequently embarrasses me fighting at the dog park is the present manifestation of this friendship. He detests being charged by inexperienced puppies, a propensity for small children to tug at his teddy bear-like ears, and the audacity of passersby to believe he will indulge them in a pet. He gets upset with me for not allowing him access to treats offered by others, and he once sunk his bottom canines into my right leg accidentally after facing off with a Shepard mix at Linfield University. He is also inclined to take on a very specific low-headed silent hunch when trying to manage a secret snatch of an unattended McDonald's burger abandoned in the tall grasses.

His most outstanding trait though, is the best of traveling companions. He is the Charlie of my own Charlie and Me (Steinbeck) ongoing adventure series. I joke with my wife that he has been to more roadside attractions, more backwoods trails, more Saturday Markets, than she and I have visited going on thirty years. He is truly the superstar of the family, still attracting people from across the street to pet him, or causing others to slow down in their trucks, just to smile as he strolls by. Passing the age of twelve, he is wily as ever, just as likely to duck his head as let you touch him once he's determined there are no hidden treats in your pocket.

Barleybear

They have been a very full twelve years. Every day of them spent in the consciousness of the terrible twos, as I am told this best represents their intellectual capacity. What has evolved is his propensity to collect nicknames; Mr. B, Sir Barles, Barley vou France', Screamer (his reaction to being alone), Snifflewick, Sir Barlington Nose Wiffer, The Wampa, Tibetan Yeti-bear, and Christopher Rubbins to share just one two-year stretch of name-calling. In his old age, we have finally decided to go with "Bubba" as his final official family nickname. Something comforting and friendly for my pal of many years. With his "big slowdown" the past two years, my wife and I have had to face the inevitable, that Wheaten Terriers do not in fact, live forever. I must say I openly disagree with God on this one. There is no joy like the joy of a Wheaten greeting you upon your return home. Barleybear bucks like a rodeo horse, smiles like a Cheshire Cat, and trots around clicking his trimmed black claws like a center ring act at the circus. He attracts crowds, stuffing his fluffy head out the drivers' side window whenever I pick up food or medication, causing others to gather in the window to see him. I promise him when he stares at me each evening while I eat one of his favorites, a salmon filet with potatoes, that if Heaven exists, he will get half of everything I eat as compensation for the torture he endured during his time on earth. For now, we must very carefully control his diet, which besides fighting, has driven him toward a constant state searching for anything and everything that might be quickly consumed. I warn people eating near him,

"Careful, my dog wants to eat the world, don't hold that corn dog too low or you'll lose it."

Demonstrating the scale of the barrels

I have also caught him eating rotting pumpkins in the garden, crushed eggs in the garbage (gone bad), cat poop at every conceivable location, and even dirt from the planter buckets placed in the outside sun. He is conniving and covert in his pursuit for eating the world. I once observed him dig through two feet of fresh snow for an empty candy wrapper. On another occasion, he managed to hypnotize the two workers at an A & W. They handed me a separate bag of chicken fingers just for him. Anything to placate those sad brown eyes and get him smiling again.

Perhaps it is my adventure co-pilot though, who will forever be stuck in my memory for his antics and companionship. Once he jumps in the car and we drive through the small town of Amity with his snout diligently stuck out the window, he knows he's in for an adventure and politely curls up on the floor behind me to sleep. When we arrive, if he isn't happy with the place, or the potential distance we'll be walking, he'll drop his butt and anchor to the spot. He then will look up casually with a stubborn expression as if to say,

"I'm not walking one more step you damn dirty ape as I don't smell one cat poop within a mile of this place, and I'm certainly not walking all the way to the pier without an incentive!"

Our relationship has become a battle of old men. I pull like a sixth grader caught in a tug-of-war match to persuade him my way, only to have him disagree and sit his butt down again.His superstar status has come to bore him, reminding me of my siblings on vacation at Disneyland, unwilling to do anything unless it involved food.

"I don't WANT to pose for another photo dad! I've had enough of this place and aren't the two-hundred photos you've already taken enough!?"

Unfortunately, he's an only child, so I need him to show the scale of the barrels at the brewpub or use his bright white fur to make the yellow leaves pop under a fall tree. It has become a bit of a game between us. He yawns bored after I manage to make him sit, and I make every possible squeak, honk or finger snap in order to have him look at me. In the end, I usually get my way and he can get back to his job of sniffing, ordering, and possibly eating the entire expanse of the earth after I take my photo.

I'm tired dad!

Chapter 6

Far Corners

"Traveling. It leaves you speechless,
then turns you into a storyteller."
-Ibn Battuta

La Grande

As mentioned in my opening, La Grande is the point in history where the strands of my family meet. Cove is a small farming community just east, where a trip with my mother is like having a map to celebrity homes in Hollywood. Every corner has a story. The boxy tavern with a strong lean is where mom once shared a beer with two of my great uncles who were the black sheep of the family. My grandmother sat waiting in the car, too proud to interact with such hillbillies after marrying into money. Walking distance from the old bar, sits a family founded church at the center of town formerly known as French Church, once holding several vestige artifacts from my early pioneer kin. A short drive to Cove Hot Springs will

bring you near the large Ponderosa Pine where mom used to tie up her horse after riding bareback to the springs for a soothing soak. I never spent more than a few days visiting Grandmother in La Grande as a child, most of it chasing three-inch grasshoppers, but there is something

about the ghosts of family footsteps that continue to bring back the rattling chains of the past. The dry fields and forested uplands speak of simpler times. Coffee mugs and overalls from a time when men raised barns and women cooked meals from scratch. All of it made with home grown ingredients. Grandmother told me that once her little brother Orville turned four,

she was told that it would be her job to raise him into adulthood. She'd also been handed the duty, at age four, to stand on the open door of the wood stove to cook breakfast for field hands. She also spoke of Native Americans stopping by for dinner, playing hooky on the local stream like Tom Sawyer, writing for the local paper, and hobos passing through town during the Great Depression. There was something magic about those times, possibly the feelings of community that ran like a deep, anchoring spine through mainstreet. I won't pretend racism wasn't prevalent at the time, but I am hopeful small communities will own up to such nonsense and strive to do better.

My last visit had taken place on an early morning in November, when the dry rounded hills to the east were layered in sparkling frost, glimmering like the lights of some far-off mythical fairy town. The farmed acres were quiet now, free from the crews of harvest, with cold-engine tractors and irrigation pipe spread near the corners of each plot. The city itself was much the same as it had been during my mother's time as a twirling band majorette in the 1950's. The ice cream shop and hamburger drive-in remain iconic for how I envision those times in my mind. Sort of a back-up set for the Happy Days television show of the 70's. What had changed, as my mother pointed out after a visit to Safeway, was the short haircuts and ties so common to her classmates were now replaced with gray sweatpants, sleeveless t-shirts, and unkempt hair. It was as if innocence itself had somehow been sucked out of the young people here. Even traditional rural counties it turns out, are not buffered from rapid changes flowing in from the outside. I'm grateful for a family history that is already baked into the cake.

Before leaving, I found myself near the barn my uncles had raised so many years before. I parked staring up at The Big, and Little Minem, small mountain ranges extending off the spine of the Rockies until halting abruptly at the edge of town. I remembered a story grandmother had told me during my teenage period as I first started going to after-dark parties in high school. Many decades before, a young Laura Richards was invited into "The Minem" as she called them, for an evening party of fiddle dancing. Being 16, she was excited to attend, but since every move had to be cleared with "Papa" beforehand, her prospects seemed dim as the sunset faded off the horizon. Finally, in an effort to frustrate her, he announced she could indeed attend the Minem party if and when she finished cleaning all of the cooking pots and dishes stacked in the sink from dinner. A mound of aluminum that might have dissuaded Cinderella from putting on her ball gown. Stubbornness, a family trait, came to the rescue, for after rolling up her sleeves she power cleaned that stack of dishes without so much as a wand wave from a fairy godmother! So, it was she stormed off angrily to be consumed by the blackest of a starless country night. Since this was around 1920, there were no easily

carried flashlights to light the trail or cell phone google apps to track her path. She recalled that as she neared the peak of the winding hilly course, she was forced to feel her way along the rockface of the south end. Progress was slow, and she didn't reach the party until late into the evening, but was triumphant. By the time she was danced out and ready to head home, she found a group of friends to lead her path home with a gas lamp. She collapsed in bed exhausted and relieved. It was the next day when the buzz around town made its way to the door via a local hunter. He had been up at first light hunting near that very spot cresting the hill where grandmother had so slowly felt her way over the pass some hours before. For it was there that the hunter had shot an enormous

Dufur

Historic schoolhouse

The first time I drove through Dufur we made a brief stop at the Ranger Station to find a buried cache of snacks in the back of the car. Looking around, my first inclination was to get the hell out of there. It was over a hundred degrees with a scrubby collection of spindly branched trees desperately clinging to their leaves as a few skinny, faded robins hid in their shadows. Apparently, they had never been taught to fly west one hour. In spite of our first unimpressive introduction, there would be several interesting adventures near Dufur in our future. The outpost next to nowhere, as I call it, hides some of the best isolated topography in the business. As fate would have it, a teacher friend, Brad, had grown up in the area where his family still held a number of acres and catered to his taste for hunting. He had once invited us to visit the family ranch, an offer that reached us during an unusual time. It was after two full years of global pandemic as infection numbers were finally in decline. Local meteorologists explained during a news cast that active sun flares would create the possibility for a brilliant Aurora Borealis. With the rise in elevation required to reach Dufur, beyond city lights, the phenomenon received a 7 rating for the strength of its potential visibility. I had no idea what that was relative too, but hey, it was a pretty solid 7! We quickly searched out appropriate locations for viewing when Brad texted the offer. We could use their family farm as our set up point! He'd inform his cousins not to shoot us on sight, and the best viewing would be near a historic schoolhouse! A gathering point locals had used for years to observe amazing sunsets and meteor showers.

It would be a grueling hour and a half drive pushing through Portland, but we finally reached the Columbia Gorge heading east! The sun was low in the sky, and the Gorge in Fall was a mavelous show of mixed colors within light and shadow. The rocky cliffs reflected their bright, grainy edges toward the retreating sun while dark basaltic chasms sunk into the blocky sides. The tan grasses of summer became a surreal sea of foam green as they rolled up the hills to greet the stone turning from gray purple to chocolate brown. Boulders at this time of year wear spectacular medals of orange and lime green lichen, arms spread like colorful snowflakes or

Columbia Gorge

splashes of paint. Cypress trees filled small drainages with vibrant yellow leaves weaving between the browns and oranges of old oaks standing in rank. Above, wispy waterfalls emerged between deep green Doug Fir, recently damaged by fire, but still holding their own in a pantheon of texture and color.

The turn from the Gorge lay just east of The Dalles, a river town with a beautiful towering church and a collection of small businesses waiting on a growth spurt. The lights disappeared behind us as we climbed the snaky corridor toward upland farmland. The grasses and isolation appeared perfect for a reissue cover of Willa Cather's O Pioneers novel. I'd once taken this same route on a late-night drive to Heppner, only to find a large porcupine in the middle of my lane as I rounded a corner, quills extended, ready for battle. I swerved at great velocity to avoid the thorny basketball that waddled away in my rearview mirror. One encounters many random Y's in this landscape with no indication of which way is your way. I figured Oz was down one path, the witches castle down the other, so I just chose left. I later learned that right would have taken me to White Falls State Park, a steep descent into a small valley of stepped waterfalls I'd visited years before. The left led to an almost abandoned stretch of asphalt where low light made it difficult to distinguish road from shoulder. The 30-foot drop was inches from the edge, almost certain death, which wasn't helping my wife in the passenger seat.

As we neared that blip in the road called Dufur, Mount Hood appeared off to the west with orange covered shoulders and what appeared to be scoops of mashed potatoes plopped on top. I pulled over to Ooo and Aaah near a boxy old barn sitting on a stream bed.

Columbia Gorge on the drive to Dufur

I admired the young trees staggering up its banks in a bid for survival. Since I normally only see Mt. Hood from its Western side, it felt like I'd reunited with an old friend who was acting neurotically. It just seemed wrong, no matter how beautiful.

Moving on, we ventured past a small collection of homes that made it officially Dufur, and we finally reached the sage covered uplands. Unfortunately, clouds had moved in, dampening our spirits for seeing the Aurora Borealis, as local news reported the phenomenon would only appear along a 7% arc above the horizon. The good news was we were in sight of the beautiful old schoolhouse that lay some 80 yards away in the middle of a plowed field. Deb distributed flashlights while I put on my winter gear.

Dufur schoolhouse, south of the Columbia River where Lewis and Clark traveled in 1805.

I felt like an astronaut exiting into an undiscovered terrain. The gritty rows of earth felt heavy under our thick boots. Barley still managed to dance like a low gravity space puppy of course, seeking to eat moon cow poop wherever it lay in the path of our lights. It was surreal in the way early space travel movies were surreal, a black and white isolation with an impending horror movie feel.

I poked around the moon rocks outside, watching the dog as Deb's light bounced through the interior. It looked like an astronaut investigating some sort of bizarre outer space Columbo murder mystery. We began our return toward the car once complete darkness enveloped us. We sat staring for thirty minutes at the dull azure horizon before I fell into a deep sleep. I drifted into some kind of weird sci-fi Dune dream on Mars until I woke up with a start. I seriously expected to find myself sitting in a rover. We were both disappointed at not seeing the Aurora Borealis of course, as this rounded out about twenty trips where we'd dedicated a chunk of time for a high probability magnetic sky. It did, however, fuel my taste for even more random adventure getaways in our state. We drove home as coyotes hunted mice along the roadside. Sweet.

Steens

Farther south, you'll find what is often referred to as "Oregon's Outback" in the dry, dusty southeast corner of the state. By the time you reach Frenchglen, you'll be ready for a stop at Fields' Station, a spot now known for its milkshakes. In earlier times, it was known for its inside joke of a handwritten "hamburgers served" board hanging on the south wall, apparently mocking McDonald's. Our first visit was in the 1990's after experiencing a shredded flat tire south of Burns, not sure we'd survive as we searched for the tire iron. We found it of course, but the entire time we wrestled with that flat, we enjoyed being peppered by the infamous country wave from passing farm workers. One of the reasons we wanted to visit the legendary **Steens Mountain** region was due to the charm of being waved at by every possible passerby. We chatted about it with a nice fellow in a cowboy hat, sitting at the Field's Station counter, before moving on to find a campsite near the mountain.

As you approach Steens Mountain from the west, you'll notice a slight rise in the landscape as you enter juniper country. There is nothing like the smell of a juniper or Ponderosa Pine forest on a sunny summer morning. Windows down, we made it to the Riddle Brothers Ranch, settled by three bachelor brothers who raised cattle in the early twentieth century. We pulled in and began to have a look around when we were greeted by a very enthusiastic summer caretaker who spent most of his year working as a college professor in Bend. I believe he mentioned it was his seventh year as caretaker just before he invited us to visit the Little Blitzen out back. Sadly, the Little Blitzen was not the progeny of Santa's reindeer, but an ankle-deep watercourse, occasionally pooling in summer to provide a much-needed place for a refreshing dip. As you learn traveling the state, many swim or soak in hot springs naked in the backcountry, a lesson learned while soaking near Hart Mountain with an older Native American gentleman. He recalled a visit from the Governor in the 1970's, who promptly stripped off his suit for a lengthy soak.

We set up our tent and unloaded supplies at the South Steens Campground. Not the most thrilling dusty launch pad I've ever inhabited, but a spot for sleep none-the-less. We decided to make the ascent up the Steens Mountain Loop late in the day as the long sun would make for better photos. We were thrilled to find wild horses lounging around a patch of tasty grasses before we launched up a hairpin turn, starting what would prove to be a most unexpected journey. I believe I was told there were plans to smooth the rugged section of road that made things so challenging since our last visit, but as that would completely alter the experience, I hold on to the hope it was just a rumor.

As we came upon the large, blocky river of stone and cobbles that substituted for a road, I was skeptical we'd survive this challenging stretch without breaking an axle. I stopped, pondering all the harrowing drives I'd successfully completed visiting isolated archaeological sites in Arizona, then consciously chose the thrill of experience over the depth of my fears. It was my wife's '87 red Toyota truck, an old friend for most of our far-off adventures, so, with her ok, we moved forward. I doubt there was more than a 20-foot stretch where all four corners of the car didn't raise up and bounce back down before we finished. When we encountered a particularly difficult section, my wife spotted out the side window, as I moved at a turtle pace over the terrain. The road felt like one of those boulder courses in Japan designed to give truck owners this kind of experience. There were more than a few times I held my breath, waiting for a buckling metal sound, before we emerged out the other side into a small circular field. My reward was the first pair of Horned Larks I'd ever seen in the wild, settling into the thick dust near the road to warm themselves. After surviving such a harrowing experience, time seemed to slow, and the innocent acts of birds took on an added significance.

We both felt we'd had more than enough adventure for one day, so after our return, we made a fire, cooked some food, and headed off for bed before the logs had a chance to turn to coals. I had only managed about an hours' sleep when the night stirred. I awoke hearing a large truck circling the campground as the driver appeared to be yelling my name. More confused than concerned, I emerged to find the ranch caretaker from earlier in our day, waving a six pack of Coors out his open window, giving party woops. I waved him over where we talked by the fire until the beer was gone, stories were exchanged, and my watch read 1 a.m. It was during that time I happened to mention our stop at Field's Station earlier in the day. He came to life and asked,

"Did you happen to see a guy in a cowboy hat sitting at the front counter?"

"Yes, we did, in fact, we talked to him for a few minutes. Why?"

"Well, back in 1968 when my hair was down to my ass, I lost a tire about a half mile up the road, so I went in for breakfast while some guy repaired it. I didn't really think about who was in the place at that time until I returned some twenty years later when I started working here summers. That guy in the hat looked at me, and I swear this is true, said, *aren't you that guy who had a tire issue back in 1968?*"

What an interesting world we live in.

As I finished this chapter, I thought about my motivation for sharing these thoughts and adventures when I'm not part of the tourist industry or any travel board. I decided my experiences speak to that place of joy we all crave outside our usual routines. A joy that comes to me by seeing life through a series of small adventures. No scheduled tours, just exploring and interacting with whoever crosses my path as I attempt to gain some perspective of place. I sometimes take issue with travel shows that give away every small-town secret or trail just for the sake of material. This tends to kill the best part of a self-directed discovery tour in my opinion. The excitement I feel finding a restaurant or backwoods hike on my own is such a rush compared to marking off a checklist. Your ability to experience a place in 360 degrees requires patience and an instinct for risking a conversation when you feel it. That's why I didn't conclude my chapter with a list of amazing little places I've visited. Sometimes you have to trust yourself to really get to the good stuff. Life is a contact sport, not in an ego way, bragging about how many cities you visited in two weeks, but using your wits and curiosity as the driving force to know exactly what is down that side alley.

John Day

I honestly do not remember the name of the campground, but when we entered John Day that early August morning, it felt like a place a wagon train had once broken down before building a town. The gardens were covered with the deer nets as we passed straight through on our way to the Strawberry Mountains. If we were in search of isolation, that is exactly what we got. A porcupine waddled across the road at one point causing us to pull over and investigate. He was so confident in his ability to ward us off, he didn't even raise his quills when we got within ten feet of him. What he did do was turn, raise his head, bare his huge, curved orange teeth before releasing a hiss that sounded like a hooded cobra ready to eat. We got the message and retreated to watch him easily climb over fallen old growth trees like they were kindergarten steps.

So, it probably wasn't the best decision to choose a campground where we were the only ones setting up a camp. We normally don't choose spots with such thick brush near the fire ring for obvious reasons, but the creek was slow and lazy and seemed to offer some good wildlife viewing. We set up our tent, did our usual exploring, then got settled in by sunset, ready to make some s'mores and watch the wood burn down to coals.

It must have been around 10 p.m., as the moon was just rising above the treetops, when something unexpected happened. One moment where there had been chirping crickets, there was a sudden burst of sound coming from the west. The brush was alive with movement and approaching fast. The sound seemed to be spread in a semi-circle, heading directly for us in one hell of a hurry. Judging by the fierce snapping of twigs and the woosh! of passing through them, there were multiple large animals attracted by our small fire. Deb and I stood up and began looking for anything that might serve as a weapon. I grabbed a lengthy section of branch burning at one end from the fire pit, as Deb picked up a large cobble for defense. The sound grew in intensity and speed, still heading right for us when it happened.

The brush line near the edge of camp, where light turned to shadow, suddenly erupted with large animals emerging from the darkness! Eight deer split and circled around our fire as we stood there open-mouthed and dumbfounded. Upon running past us, just as suddenly, they stopped in their tracks, turning to stare back into the shrubs. I instinctively turned on my flashlight and pointed it into what I claim to this day, was the brief reflection of yellow eyes prowling ten feet beyond the shrub line. My wife disagrees of course, but it would have been consistent with what the deer did next. As they continued focusing their eyes back to where they had emerged, they all, one after another, knelt down and plopped around the fire for about ten minutes. It was consistent with my theory. They were being chased by a cougar, saw the fire, and hoped to use the cougar's fear of fire against it. For an animal that is not given much credit for its brains, I think it was a very successful plan. Although, I'm not really happy about what the result might have been if the predator had decided to stroll into camp after them.

Fisherman's bend near Mill City
Santiam River

Chapter 7

A World All Its Own

"Portland, Oregon won't build a mile
of road without a mile of bike path."

-Lance Armstrong

Portland

Portland is the elephant in the room when it comes to experiencing Oregon. I can't tell you how many states I've explored across the Midwest where I've thought, oh, this is like Eugene, or this has a Pendleton vibe, only to be left with, they have no Portland! It's become almost cliché' when I meet people traveling once they learn I'm from just outside Portland. They always, and I mean always, say, "OH! I'm going to live there someday!" As for new arrivals who choose to join us here, there is one thing you should know before you unpack the suitcase. *Portland is a city you either love or hate; there is no gray area.*

Based on exit interviews with relatives who left years ago, this largely depends on your politics, tolerance to diversity, aversion to weirdness, and ability to participate in very random conversations. I once found myself in a circle of local farmers a mere thirty miles outside of the city as one after another declared,

Portland mural

"I HATE Portland." To which I replied, "Then it is probably not for you."

Chances are, if you like to wear black, use very expensive alternatives to cars for commuting, feign an artistic background, own a $3,000 bike, hangout at any number of pubs after 5 p.m. three to six days a week, don't blink at a twenty-minute wait for a latte, Portland probably IS for you. There is Old Mystical Portland which still clings to the fringes. Those charming little places like the Dan and Louis Oyster Bar off SW Ankeny, Powell's Books, the Portland Zoo, the Japanese Garden, Hippo Hardware, the Rhododendron Garden near Reed College, Oaks Park, all nestled between numerous incredible walks through beautiful neighborhoods. New Portland includes theme bars, vegan pool halls, Blue Star Donuts, Tilikum crossing, and Ken's Artisan Pizza. I can't remember a time parking my car in Portland where a walk didn't turn into an interesting adventure. An accidentally found rose garden, a street person yelling poetry at parked cars about trains, and the colorful spray-painted street art on the exterior of a bar wall were all experiences I had during a recent walk. Inside Hippo Hardware, I might spend a full ten minutes staring at Victorian door knobs before buying a t-shirt. Just south on Mississippi Avenue, I empathize with the locals who spray paint obscenities on the new expensive apartment complexes being flash built there. But somehow, Portland against all odds, remains uniquely weird and interesting.

Portland church near PSU

Protests and Riots

Art and graffiti pay tribute to victims of race related violence

Coming in from rural farm country 35 miles outside Portland, you can imagine how the protests that erupted after George Floyd's murder created exaggeration and misunderstanding within that community. While Donald fumed at Portland's Mayor, acquaintances from all over the country texted links about the terror that had seized Portland through unruly mobs taking control of the streets. Some even claimed the city was razed to the ground by radical anarchists intent on ending civilization. After much rumor and hyperbole, I decided a day trip was necessary just a week after the most violent period. I wanted to see for myself exactly

who these "radical terrorists" were and the damage they were capable of inflicting.

I mapped out parking the day before, ensuring the Federal courthouse, where most news coverage originated, would be my center point. I packed a fully charged cell phone, some snacks, and a healthy sense of trepidation.

My wife and I slipped into the city like a scouting party, landing a block from the epicenter cautiously. The concrete was cold, the air damp and heavy. We heard a few distant honks with only one casual passerby. Right away, I noticed it wasn't the Portland I'd known since my return. It was too quiet, as if we'd touched down in a foreign country on holiday. This felt like hibernation, the tourists long gone, and you could feel a stark contrast between police and the protesters everywhere. A police car would cruise by, lights flashing, leaving us among sleepy protestors camped in the park starting breakfast. The Apple store and Dolce & Gabbana, which had been the target of the early protests, were boarded up with large sheets of plywood. These were destined to become canvases of tribute to those who had fallen victim to race related violence. Breanna Taylor and George Floyd, among many others, were depicted in peaceful repose, challenging the observer to take a stand and say their name. I was neither beaten, nor confronted. We took our time carefully examining the artworks while the majority seemed to quick step their way past, intent on their destinations. It was a very different experience.

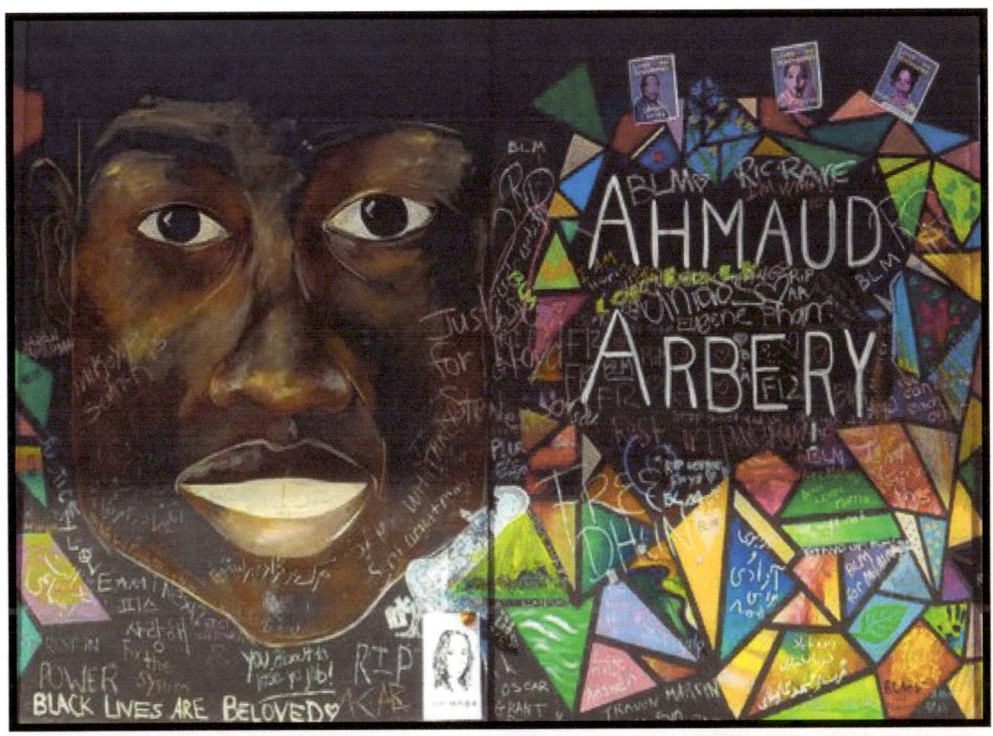

The Pandemic

It was February when the schools closed, and everyone knew we were in for a bumpy ride. With the spring, and a lengthy lock down into summer, suddenly hand sanitizer and toilet paper disappeared from shelves and things turned to an attitude of every man for himself. Members in my extended family had immune system challenges or were well within their golden years, so masks and social distancing became the standard. Getting into a masking routine was definitely a challenge as I'd often find myself halfway across a grocery store parking lot before realizing I'd left my mask in the glove compartment. I wear glasses when driving, so I'd have to always remove them to avoid fogging up. Soon, I developed some steps; I'd roll up my mask in a side pocket, leave my glasses on the dash, then place my cell in a coat pocket. Honestly, it was a pain in the butt, but rather than infecting someone's grandparent or small child with a possibly fatal virus, I exchanged a little inconvenience for the peace of mind of safety. I just couldn't live with killing someone if a piece of cloth might prevent it.

Doing my part to be safe

So, if there is one thing that really stood out over the two years of a worldwide pandemic, it was how divided we became over such a simple act as masking. This was the first time I'd seen such a divide so visibly in my normally mellow state of Oregon. When mom and I had stopped for gas in Pendleton, the gas attendant was offended we were masked while handing him our credit card, even after admitting he thought he'd had covid the previous week. Mom is in her eighties. My visit to the Columbia Gorge Model Train club was even more bizarre as a man waiting at the door became so incensed after a polite request to mask up his six-year-old son, he kept pointing skyward yelling,

"He will judge, he will judge!"

When I walked in, I noticed 80% of the people attending were over 75 years of age. Oregon reflects our national division which will continue being a problem until we can begin listening again.

Empty shelves became a norm

Living With Forest Fires

Back door lock

It was during the Labor Day weekend of 2020 when local news reported a powerful wind descending into the Willamette Valley out of the east. It was unclear why this deserved so much attention as warm winds were not an oddity during a Pacific Northwest summer, but the danger revealed itself soon after arriving. The wind was fierce, and according to one report, sent a dangling trailer hitch chain across the pavement in a shower of spark. It quickly ignited dry grasses nearby. A downed power line also contributed to the scattered pockets of flame soon turning into islands of fire. Most of the Cascade Range, a line of active volcanoes, received the brunt of the devastation. Looking eastward from the low hills of the farm, a massive bulb of dark clouds rose skyward, as if an atomic bomb were dropped into the wilderness. Before long they transformed into large red-gray masses of soot moving slowly overhead turning day into night. For three days, everything was saturated in an eerie twilight. Clouds extended from ground to altitude. They lumbered toward the coast, slowly digesting the blue of the horizon. The early arrivals soon turned to a gritty gray ash toxic brew that settled between the trees and earth, got into eyes, and ground between teeth. As quickly as that, Covid-19 and protest went to the back pages. Just a couple minutes gathering firewood from the garage led to burning lungs, and the back door lock soon became encrusted by an odd mustard colored coating. But even as our world became surrounded in charcoal, a single white rose bloomed at the back of the yard.

Living in Fire

From ashes comes beauty

Distant plumes form the horizon.

A warm eastern wind howls…

As a red wolf stalks the forest.

Thick, dark death rolls skyward

Flashing lights surround islands of orange

A Mars like delusion bathes me

In ethereal red-yellow twilight.

Trees, grasses, homes, animals…

Seek the sea drifting overhead.

Bags, antiques, my guitar sit at the door…

A filthy grit between teeth.

Roses sit silent; depressed…dusted…done.

A fresh bloom dare press through

Held in the dying arms of others.

From the ashes, love finds a home.

Fishermen's Bend three days before the fire ravaged it

From the ashes......

Comes new life.

Richard Kofford
1933 - 1983

He always used to tell me, half of life is just showing up!

A Father's Time Capsule

It was mid-Fall not long after the forest fires were contained. The ravaged Cascades knocked upon the door of Salem after gobbling several small towns along the way. Highway 22 connecting Salem and Bend was closed for months as the smoldering remnants of torn lives and felled trees were inspected and cleared. When the all-clear came on local news, I wanted to see the damage firsthand, and planned a trip to the small city of Sisters where I'd meet my brother for breakfast at a local café. Covid levels were all over the place at that time; high one day, plummeting the next, but something compelled me to go. Maybe it was my inspiring visit to "Fisherman's Pass" on the Santiam River, or the stop in Mill City for a burger three days before fire obliterated the area. I needed to see the extent of the devastation for it to be real, and if time, see if a sacred family camp site in the deep woods near a Lake had survived the recent crisis.

My first attempt to drive out was on an early Tuesday morning. It was a few days after the highway reopened and I was out of bed and off by 6:15 a.m. Hot tea in hand, I felt good about the day as I drove past the capitol building in Salem. It was bad luck that another easterly wind, this time a freezing one, had dropped out of Alberta to rattle the landscape charging down the West Cascades. I'd stop in Mill City as before, but this time I sat within a landscape of fire. I noticed how selective the flames had been while snaking through the area like a Moses plague. Rosie's, a traditional scone stop, stood firm and undamaged ten feet off the road, while several homes behind the business were nothing but twisted metal and ash. It took a few moments for the damage to sink in. Rust colored trucks with melted tires sat abandoned, as a burnt hedge, singed within four feet of Rosie's back corner, told the story of the flames. Clearly it was a restless evening for all, but just the preliminary for what I'd find down the road in Detroit.

Cottonwood Cafe

In that city, a torched fire truck sat in the middle of downtown, overwhelmed by heat before being abandoned within eyeshot of the isolated chimneys that now looked like skinny tombstones. It was around Idahna that I began to notice a change in the wind, when branches started accumulating in the road and hitting my hood. Without the windbreak of the forest, the air grew icy, numbing fingers quickly when I stopped for a few photos. Soon after the air grew heavy with the smell of sulfur and that was it. I turned around. My brother was disappointed, so I agreed to try again in a few days after the freak winds passed.

On the following Friday, I made sure to leave after 8:00 a.m. to ensure the sun would begin melting any road ice by the time I reached the mountains. There was no need to worry as a steady rain kicked in soon after leaving Salem. The trip went smoothly though Mt. Washington, and much of the Santiam Pass was obscured by fog, delaying my arrival in Sisters by a half hour. Marc and I pulled up outside the Cottonwood Café approximately thirty seconds and one hundred feet apart. Our meeting originally was to be a check in, but as the Café was abandoned, and the food delivered in record time, we agreed that rain was no deterrent for driving up to the lake to check out our old haunts and talk about our memories of dad, who died not long after his fiftieth birthday.

When I was 12, dad and I went camping about a mile from Three Creeks Lake, at what we always referred to as, "The Little Lake." Along with five other families, we set up our tent in between the tightly packed trailers for ten days of relaxation. My best friend and I looked forward to these trips all year as we explored mountain slopes with bb guns, chased trout, and target shot. We learned how to chop up firewood with our hatchets and make a fire with just a few sticks and paper. We gained confidence in ourselves in the wilderness and learned responsibility communally. For dad, it was the chance to leave his principal role behind to fix food over hot coals and enjoy the occasional round of Frisbee bowling with friends. That entire summer he wore his beat-up, faded cowboy boots which had deteriorated from cedar red into a buckskin blonde over the previous decade. It was during our final day in camp that something compelled him to make a statement about what a great summer we'd had. He removed his left boot, seizing a long tent spike before climbing atop the old green station wagon, hammering it into the side of a pine tree. Others around the camp laughed openly, finding it a ridiculous gesture when there were much more interesting things to do. As it turned out, that would be our last year to camp at the Little Lake, and my father would die unexpectedly eight years later. My teen years had drawn me away from the precious family time we had enjoyed.

"The way I see it, we have a one in a million shot at finding that old boot out there, but I want to give it a try," he said. I nodded, waved the waitress over for the bill, and pulled on my coat.

We drove up the southbound road into the Sister's Wilderness area, reminiscing about past trips and misadventures, when the smooth pavement became bumpy rock road. The truck bounced and lurched at an impressive five miles an hour before rounding a familiar large meadow surrounded by dwarfed alpine fir. There had been fire damage on some ridges along with a few dead tree stands, but Tam McArthur Rim was still equally majestic, and the lake, though down a few feet, was still pristine with the sagging brown boat rental house at the east end. Our main campsite was now a parking lot for a nearby trailhead, but you could still see the flattened areas dug out for the tents and trailers along with the main fire pit area. Everything seemed so much smaller to my adult brain. In grade school I thought I was camping in Switzerland, and the once isolated campsite now seemed to be crawling with hip techies loaded down with expensive gear and entitled attitudes. It was still beautiful, but much like Yosemite, was slowly being trampled into the ground by those without a similar attachment.

Michael Kofford

We searched our traditional group campsite until I was convinced I remembered correctly that the boot was originally placed at the little lake. Marc confessed he'd heard the story so many times in his post-teen years, the tale somehow managed to worm its way into his working consciousness until he believed he'd been there. Forty years later, the natural area still held a few scars from the camping it endured, but no boot. Determined to find the family relic, we gave a last sweep before loading up to find the little lake, which would test the few remaining fragments of my memory.

Marc Kofford

We slowly rolled down the pumice filled road at a 5-mph cruising speed, searching for the tiniest hint of our former camp site. About half the trees just a few hundred yards from the lake appeared to be dead or dying, making it much easier to peer farther back from the main road. Suddenly, I spotted a cluster of dark stones that triggered a memory. There was a dry, sunken spot in the landscape with large blocky blackened basaltic rock at its center, once used by sunbathers to warm themselves after swimming. It was the correct distance from the main road, so I pointed and yelled for Marc to make the next turn. With crippling knee pain from the recent cold weather, he struggled to maintain a slow pace as he turned onto a sandy side road bordering our potential campsite. He relieved himself immediately upon opening the door, but I was too anxious with the match in topography to wait. I searched my memory of the landscape as I marched to the edge of the depression where the little lake once sat. Who could forget the clear water filled with fat, little black pollywogs we hunted with bb guns. Now, there wasn't a hint of water, or the previous summers spent there. Like many, I believed the richness and variety of life was too expansive to ever be touched by the hand of man. How naïve we all were.

The blonde deadwood, stood like tombstones, the work of boring beetles aided by soaring summer temperatures brought on by global warming. It was like visiting the shell of an old burnt-out cabin after a forest fire. I wondered if the snows that visited the area December through February were enough to dampen the dusty, cracked bottom of the pond anymore. I picked up a handful of the sandy dust letting it sift through my fingertips like sugar. I scanned the desolation. I wondered if the dinosaurs felt such sadness as their world drifted away from them. Still, I did know this was the place, and encouraged my brother to join me as there might still be one last bright spot remaining.

I watched him hobble toward me, a tad impatient as I asked him to walk forty yards out from the dry rim of the lake to where I stood. We'd walk the circumference of the depression I explained, searching the trees between us as we progressed forward. He soon became occupied trying to summit a fallen snag as I continued on. It was some twenty steps later my eyes rested forward, spotting what looked like a large, shriveled mushroom emerging from the side of a tree. It was twelve feet on the east side, exactly the height of my 6'4" dad standing on the back of our green station wagon. I shook my head and narrowed my eyes, not letting hope in just yet. I made a b-line for the odd shape.

"Marc! I've found it! I yelled, smiling as I shook my head.

The Infamous Boot

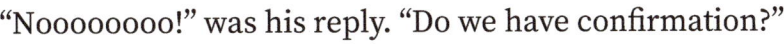

"Noooooooo!" was his reply. "Do we have confirmation?"

I walked a few steps closer until I clearly saw visible stitches on the underside of the sole.

"Yup. Confirmed."

Though the pointed toe of the boot had curled backward after decades of freezing blizzards and blistering sun. It reminded me somewhat of the Wicked Witch of the East's retreating foot after the ruby slippers had been removed by the Good Witch. The buckskin-colored leather had morphed into a sort of rubbery, walnut skinned ornament. I waited for Marc, then we walked shoulder to shoulder to the tree where my brother turned on one heel, his mouth wide open, overwhelmed by disbelief. We didn't speak a few moments, soaking in a final tie with the father who had died over forties years before. We took pictures, told stories of old campfires, then slowly drifted back to the truck where we sat silent. Finally, the car rumbled to a start as my brother looked at me.

"You know, I think dad had a hand in leading us here."

Tam McArthur Rim

Camping at Three Creeks Lake in 1970

As things turned out, Marc would only remain in the state another month before moving back to Las Vegas, leaving me to consider that lone boot howling in the wind as I sit comfortably with my tea.

Chapter 8

Back To The Farm

"Some call it the middle of nowhere.
I call it the center of my world."
-Farm Life Quotes

I have been greeted by many exciting things when walking out of this old farmhouse early each morning. One day, I emerged just in time to catch the final approach of a weary eagle lifting his feet to the top of the old sequoia out front. Another day, I found three massive flocks of Starlings shifting and moving like living clouds, moving through one another in perfect synchronization, only to dive away a moment later. Then, there was the early dawn I saw a long-tailed weasel dash ten feet in front of me before disappearing down a hole near the lilac bush. I have also found myself being circled from above by five large, red-headed Turkey vultures. I raised my hands with a query:

"Who have you come for!?" I demanded, but they just slowly drifted away once they realized the rumors of my death had been exaggerated.

Wheat field on farm

Egg wagons

For a while, I developed the habit of almost instinctively raising my cell phone during such encounters, but as time marched on, I have come to accept that in order to truly enjoy and savor such instances, one must live completely in that moment, refusing to give it away so easily. I learned in the spring, if I am up at 5:30 a.m., it is a good idea to sit on the front porch to listen to the White-Crowned Sparrow joyfully claiming his breeding territory, or to calmly sit in the front lawn to await the sun to turn the slopes of Mount Hood from blue to orange. So, it was many mornings passed.

My first spring, I walked out in my tattered gray robe to stack firewood on one arm, when suddenly two dark chevrons passed before my face at sonic speed. Oddly, it felt like

Barred owl at Tice Park in McMinnville

Fruit and Vegetables from our garden

Killdeer eggs

Batman threw something at me, but it happily turned out to be a pair of Barn Swallows returning to the farm for nesting in our garage. The evidence came from the line of woven mud already outlining the side of the support beam. Only once have I been able to observe this process up close. Standing in line for fish and chips in Nehalem, I watched a pair of swallows fly from the bank of the nearby river to the rib of a large overhead umbrella providing shade to customers. I stood completely fascinated. Each would arrive with either a beak full of mud or light grasses. They then appeared to turn their beaks sideways as they placed the first foundation layer. What they created started to look like one coil in a coiled pot. It saddened me that all their efforts would be lost at the end of the day when the umbrellas were rolled up.

In my garage, the coiled pot would be completed after two weeks. Not long after, I noticed grasses and feathers sticking over the brim, so I lifted my cell phone just high enough to take a photo. Four beautiful little eggs, light tan with dark brown splotches, were huddled together at the center of the nest. I loved to watch the two parents as I sat on the front porch. They would effortlessly weave and dive across the sky, circling like two spitfires in a deadly dogfight. The wings end in a sharp point, which they pull closer while performing a particularly challenging arc around the lilac bush. I imagine jet engineers must have considered the idea of a bendable, flexible wing after watching such birds. Their fast, light movements earn such admiration from me.

Barn swallows in my garage

Once the eggs hatch, the slightest sound of moving a tool, or grabbing kindling, will cause them to thrust their huge open mouths upward. When you see the adults sitting on a wire out front, you'd never suspect they are hiding great white shark mouths under all those feathers. There is one other characteristic that stands out even more though. The babies are dead eyes when it comes to defecating. It was the first week after I spotted their little eyes looking down at me, I began to notice a small ten-inch diameter circle of white blobs appear on the concrete floor. The young babies instinctively lean their hinnies over the edge of the nest in the same direction and fire at will, always keeping a set distance. It's like they are born with their own shovel and bucket to keep the nest clean.

The Turkey Vultures arrive like clockwork. These prehistoric looking throwbacks stand in the fields their first few days back, as if looking for a mastodon stuck in the mud. Their bulky bodies take lots of energy to unfold and flap skyward, so they hop around the ground, waiting on the tractors fire up signaling the first spring plowing. As Great Blue Herons stab at frogs with their spear-like beaks, and the Northern Harriers sweep a few feet over the ground in search of unwary mice, the vultures pick over the plowed furrows to snatch the easy pickings raised by the blades. It looks a bit gruesome watching from the sidelines, but nature doesn't seem to take as kindly to waste as we do. Vultures are basically nature's garbage cans, but no pulling out to the curb.

I admit it, I do not like Starlings. They will pick my bird feeders clean in a single day, create messy nests made of large twigs big enough for an eagle, and take no care about where they direct their poop. They do, however, possess one phenomenal characteristic I do admire. They are incredible parents. It does not matter how big the predator, how sharp the claws, Starling parents fearlessly jump into action upon spotting Bald Eagles, Red Tailed Hawks, or harriers to chase them off. They will follow these predators well away from the nest until they are sure the message is received and not forgotten. This explains part of the problem why this European bird has adapted so thoroughly to our climate and continues to dominate the landscape.

It was in 2020, just before the pandemic began, my wife's sister announced a surprise visit to the farm from Vermont. She explained she needed a break from running the family business in the confines of the log cabin they also lived in. Winters are mind-numbingly long in the North Country, and after spending ten years living 50 miles from the Canadian border, I can tell you it's a whole new dimension of cabin fever. Being an educated biology college professor, I inevitably found her at the edge of my garden soon after arriving. She perused our randomly planted tomatoes, squash, cucumbers, pumpkins, and rows of lettuce, easily identifying each even before fruiting. I was curious how one tiny head of lettuce failed to grow as the one next to it flourished, as they shared equal amounts of nutrients, sun, and water. She explained it as genetic variability. Some plants, just like animals, possess a flaw that might be beneficial under changing circumstances. If the soil became more acidic, colder on average, or dryer, the presently wilting failure might become the dominant strain. In a world of quickly changing environments, this rolling of genetic dice may potentially lead to big dividends, or a fade into obscurity.

My favorite moment from her stay came when she rose from our two-day discussion at the kitchen table to head out to the garden with a pair of snub-nosed scissors. There she clipped a palm full of the much-maligned kale before carefully gathering the remaining ingredients for our meal, prepared as follows:

Sizzle minced garlic in a large pan in cold-pressed olive oil.

Add the kale and pour a bit more olive oil on top before stirring vigorously on medium heat.

Add shredded carrots (fresher the better), sun-dried tomatoes (ours were store bought),
other vegetables to taste, before serving with thinly sliced cucumbers on top.

Farm fresh salad

Apple picking

Items from our garden

Blueberries from nearby farm

Cherries from our farm

Asian pears on the farm

Strawberry picking

Peaches

Vineyard

Apple picking ladder

Cherry blossoms

Caterpillar

Yellow flowers near Amity

I know friends in big cities who grow very respectable gardens, but there is no feeling quite like living on a farm and serving up a hot, steaming stir fry thirty minutes after you have harvested the majority of the ingredients fifty feet away.

A few other favorite moments I'd like to include:

1. Hearing what sounded like someone snapping a flag, only to see a Red-Tailed Hawk turning in a dive to buzz a landed Bald Eagle hunched over a raccoon carcass.

2. Seeing all the Barn Swallow babies sitting on nails in the garage just before taking their first flight with mom and dad.

3. As I watered our roses on a hot summer day, a hummingbird suddenly appeared at the end of the hose five inches from my hand for a drink of water, dipping his beak in and out of the stream.

4. Hearing the Great Horned Owls, on three sides of the house, trying to out "who" the others.

5. The fact that Red Cedars sprout like weeds here.

6. That split second you lock eyes with a wild coyote before it turns to run.

Oregon pear

Low sun shimmers off the farm pond

Remnants of an icestorm

Farm pond

Out for a walk

Bounties from the farm

Real or Fake?

At this point, I'd like to introduce a game I like to play with my city friends. It is called, real or fake. I will send them a photo of a small section of stream that is either a fake stretch of stream sitting in front of a corporate headquarters, or a wild one a few miles from the farm. They must respond within ten minutes with "Real," or "Fake," to be awarded points. See how you can do.

The Eclipse, The Sky, and Wonder

My day began that August 21st, 2017, driving into the small town of Amity to get a hot tea before a walk with my dog. The first time ever, I found a traffic jam extending a half mile outside the city in both directions. Half the plates were from California and Washington, but a few came from even farther. Just then my cousin Erick called me from my moms' beach house. It was full eclipse day, and every New Age spiritualist was armed and dangerous with rechargeable quartz crystals. He asked if he and his oldest son could view the eclipse from the farm. Apparently, the full eclipse would only last 30 seconds at the coast, while ours would graciously submit to over two minutes. He arrived with a hug and set to work preparing his tripod as Deb and I donned our geeky cardboard viewing glasses. We were soon invited to hike up the hill and join the farmer and his extended family where they had set up a small buffet with a mimosa vodka station. My cousin grew up in Manhattan, so it was kind of like entering Willy Wonka's Chocolate River room when he saw the giant pigs, penned goats, and two show cows, the pride of the farmer's daughter's grandchildren at the state fair. We were two-thirds through the eclipse process when suddenly everyone on the highway below just pulled over. Every farm entrance, every small gravel patch, held a minivan filled with people gawking out their windows. As the eerie twilight darkness fell over the land, the crows and vultures took flight, circling the fields, looking for a place to roost. There was something very Texas Chainsaw Murder about it, but after things settled, there was a very cosmic peace to the whole thing. It was gone as quick as it had come, and so were the mini-vans and new age travelers.

When you only have one light on a telephone pole over 360 acres, it is only a short walk to look up and see the Milky Way. If you have ever looked out your plane window late at night to see that one point of light below, that's us. It has allowed for some pretty memorable viewing experiences in our five years here. For me, I would have to say the Super Flower Blood Moon would be the most spectacular. We nearly missed it because it was hiding behind the giant sequoia in the front lawn. It was only because we got frustrated that we ran outside and started looking around. What really stopped me in my tracks over this rare phenomenon, was how

the moon suddenly took on a three-dimensional appearance. It looked as if I could reach up, bounce the moon like a ball for a few minutes, before throwing it back up into the night sky. The vibrant soft peachy-red made it appear more like a background prop at Disneyland than our typical moon. Of the two, this was clearly my favorite over the Wolf Blood Moon we'd soon add to our viewing collection, which appeared both brighter and flatter.

Then there was NEOWISE, the fuzzy snowball comet that raced across our skies, visiting earth in July of 2020. What truly amazed me about all of the spectacular sky show experiences was how few of my friends even bothered to go outside. On several occasions, I'd call friends to make sure they didn't miss the once in a lifetime opportunity, only to learn they were watching tv. I'd tell them where to look in the sky, and sure enough, all of them were blown away after simply walking outside. I've been in many full auditoriums for light shows, but when it comes to the free, natural ones, so many seem to pass. That night, we walked up into the plum orchard and searched the night sky until locating it. I'll never forget that feeling of wonder that hit me as NEOWISE sat in the blackness above me. I knew, long after I was gone, that comet would continue passing by the earth, to attract eyes that haven't even been born yet. So maybe that is why I have always been so intrigued by the stars beyond their beauty. Their omnipresence is our connection to eternity, while sitting on this grain of sand, lost in a sea of cosmic dust. I don't feel young or old when I look up at the night sky, I just

feel a part of it. There is peace in that oneness.

As I near the end of this book, I think of all the adventures I neglected to mention. Looking at Jupiter through the Pine Mountain observatory telescope, the early morning fishing trips with dad to Olallie Lake below Mount Jefferson, Crater Lake trips, are among many I have left out. There are still things that remain on my list. Search for Sun Stones, our state rock, near the California border, dig for clams in Netarts Bay, possibly deep-sea fish for salmon, to name a few. Most of all, I'm grateful for growing up here, able to return again and again after venturing to other parts of America. Every state has its particular brand of beauty, but I could never replace the tall trees and green grasses of Oregon because they have deep roots in my heart.

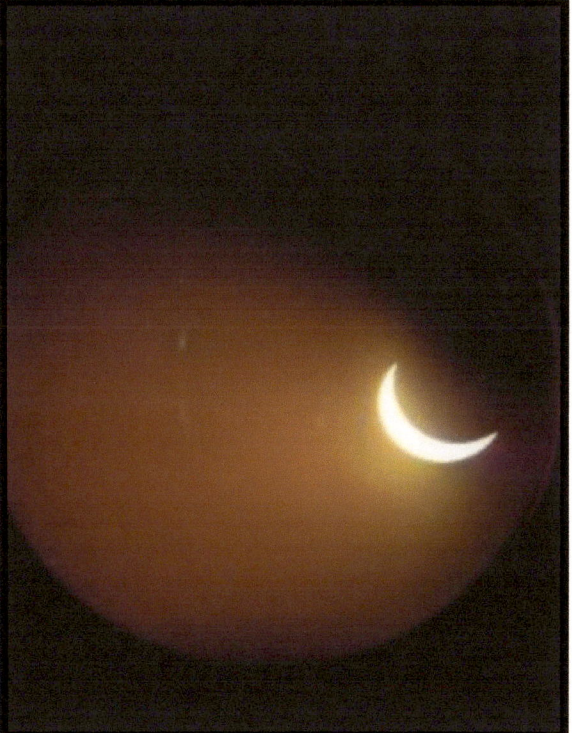

The 2017 Eclipse

Gratitude

When I walk the fields
and observe the storm,
Gratitude flows
As a timeless well
into a loving stream.
For the Crowned Sparrows
who woke me at first light.
The roses and the falcons,
The stones from distant mountains.
An early morning fog
Clinging to a spider web,
Before rain drenches clothes
Standing in the orchard.
A land brought to life
from volcano fire.
Please, angry cold ocean
Take my ashes and sweep them
Into your blue heart.
Let the dust devils spin them,
The waves grind them,
The rivers carry them,
And the plums grow from them.
Oregon, I was proud to know you
A ride sweet as wine.

Chapter 9

Just Because

""If we were meant to stay in one place,
we'd have roots instead of feet."

- Rachel Wolch

Unique & Interesting

UFO Parade in McMinnville

Dragon Boat Finish 2022

Fish made from discarded plastics in Lincoln City

Snail on Darrow Park trail near Salem

Foggy Oaks

146 OREGON

Manzanita Beach

Old barn near Dayton

Passing clouds

Frisbee golf course near Salem

Wigwam burner

5th Street Market in Eugene

Salem Castle

Willamette Queen in Salem

Carousel in Riverfont Park, Salem

Art stone in McMinnville

Artwork on Linfield campus

Grandpa's ladder

Sasquatch...Myth?

East Portland church tower

Deep Wood Mansion

University Festival

Near downtown Salem

Native dancers at Grand Ronde Pow Wow

Native American tools and artifacts

Ride the rails near Wheeler

St. John's grape stomping festival

Mailboxes by Newberg Cultural Center

Daisies

Huey is a Vietnam memorial in Canby

Herbert Hoover's boyhood home in Newberg

Live action reading

Church towers in Ellwood

Lewis and Clark State Park

Newberg, OR

Japanese Garden

Salem waterfront

Love locks near the Grain Station restaurant

Stairs in Newberg

"Heiser Farm" where the corn maze is located

Driftwood fence

Tulips in the sun

Octopus Hotel

Observatory building

Kris at Erratic Rock

Kris's greenhouse

Linfield University

Hoisting a brew at the Taphouse

Jacksonville City Hall

Linfield University

Night Lights

Zoo Lights

Zoo Lights

Zoo Lights

Artistic Lights

Zoo Lights

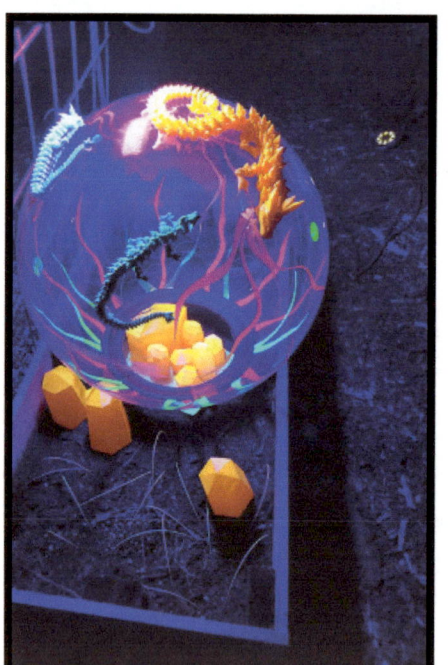

Winter

Light

Festival

Christmas lights in Cottage Grove

Garden castle Christmas lights

Cottage Grove Christmas lights

Tunnel lights in Cottage Grove

When a House Becomes a Home

There is a small town south of the bursting coastal community of Cannon Beach where my mother lives. She lamented one summer,

"California found us!" as the crowd flow forced its way into the small community.

Now you must be in line by 7:10 a.m. during the summer months or suffer little hope of seeing a beverage at the coffee shop in less than an hour. And with the sun and roar of the waves so close, nothing could be more of an intolerable torture to a native Oregonian than a line. It's origins as a small hippie community which chose to build in the shadows of a Sitka Spruce forest over sixty years ago continues hanging on, but by a thread. If you visit the beach during an early pre-dawn fog, you will more than likely find locals already busily collecting the previous nights' trash. Surfers it seems, are more content with using the environment than preserving it.

Mom

Our little two-bedroom shack up on the hill was nothing special when we purchased it in 1990. My brother was awestruck by the fact that there were no windows facing the beach view. Something unheard of now.

Mom's kitchen

"Whoever built this place must have been born here," he concluded, "disgusted by the sight of a beach that had become so omni-present."

We gathered at the house one early July morning to begin the remodel process. Two of us at each corner of the upper-level roof were posted near a hydraulic press, simultaneously pumping the side handles in time. The attic was soon a master bedroom and the three walls that faced the woods and the ocean became a panoramic view. The deck was repaired and wrapped around the house and the front parking lot was turned into a blooming garden of color. The house was the

Mom's beach house

vision of my car designer stepfather, a native Oregonian, who had somehow been so altered by forty years in the auto-industry in Detroit, he thought green marble with black walls and light switches was a good idea. The front door was encased in a tall wall my brother came to refer to as the tombstone.Through thirty years within that tiny three-bedroom home we lived a second life. My niece and nephew grew from thin children into hearty adults, neighbors passed, and my birthday candles grew from one match manageable into an uncontrollable forest. When Carl died, the small, dusty crabbing boat was hauled away as a new chapter began. Our knees and backs would give out, and suddenly we felt like old men. Somehow, beautiful traditions were preserved, such as fresh halibut dinners and holiday gatherings, but as the sands of time emptied, mom was finally ready to move on. There was yet one more lesson for this house to teach us.

With the spread of drought and fire in the south, it suddenly became the norm for people driving past in BMWs to offer a million dollars for a small, unused plot. The wonderful community values by which we were raised began disappearing into "grand entrances" and blocky glass contemporary modern eyesores as a dilemma soon entered our family. Did we put an outrageous price tag on the home to ensure mom had plenty of money in her retirement, or did we side with community and make sure some massive spa resort didn't nose their way in, blocking off the view and the livability for the rest of the quiet gardeners who lived up the street. We gathered much as the Sioux did over a century ago. As thousands of settlers passed through their lands killing buffalo and searching for gold, we were left with a similar question, *what are we to do?* Almost on cue, an answer came from our neighbors who asked if they could make a bid on the house. A fair bid in line with the appraised value at the time, but a bigger question still loomed, could we pass on the additional funds that would surely result from a bidding war?

In the end, we sold it to the lovely couple from Seattle next door. They promised the trees and the habitat would stay, and the community attitude that was such a big part of small town life, would not be surrendered to some massive spa resort. So, as I look at the house now, I feel both sadness and joy.

Kite flying in the sand

Simple beauty

View from mom's deck

Pacific waves

Wall of Memories

"And into the forest I go, to lose
my mind and find my soul."
                    -John Muir

And so, as the sun rises in the East, a new day, a new adventure on the horizon...

Epilogue - Before You Move

I tend to think of community as the healthy root system of an old oak tree. The roots extend deep into the ground until reaching a firm anchor with which to create a solid foundation. A sturdiness which allows the remaining arms to reach skyward without tumbling downhill. When my grandmother reached her eighties, I used to find cupboards filled with rubber band balls, flattened cardboard boxes, old plastic bags, and carefully divided lines of crackers. It led me to questions what in her past history left such deep scars in her daily consciousness. Survivors of the Great Depression could certainly compare their depth and number with those who survived World War 2, but the scars of each age manifest differently. For a time that seems so foreign today, those scars still flow through my marrow and mark me in some ways.

"Papa," as she called him, was a word spoken with a certain firmness. After seventy years she still held a respectful fear of him. He ran the family farm with a firm hand and once made her cut a switch out of an oak tree in the front yard upon learning she'd disobeyed his instructions by jumping in the haymow. A haymow is where loose hay is stored for animals, in the upper loft of a barn. A switch being a firm stick with just the right amount of flexibility to give a lasting impression of who was boss. She lowered her britches before Papa silently dispensed a whipping that still caused her eyes to well up many years later.

Deeply felt stories are the backbone of a community, and when they are shared, they help hold together the fabric of a family, a neighborhood, and a nation.

Our tree

Looking at our tree, the bark is perhaps our buildings, homes, and schools, places that provide us the necessary security to be nurtured and develop. When I visit the Junior High School I attended, now a middle school, I still see the raucous snowball fights that took place just outside the front doors of the building. I feel the shocks that were dished out from the orange carpet as classmates rubbed their feet together before extending a finger. And those places in turn, keep a part of us.

A view from our farm

A binding energy from each successive generation which stores our memories and experiences, thus influencing how we raise our own children and treat each other.

Leaves are the values of place. They change like the seasons of life. They create the soil that keeps us steady, providing a starting point from which to grow. The strong examples set by my parents allowed me to see those values in action, like joining them one morning to volunteer at a community event. I noticed how they greeted others, how they interacted respectfully, and the way they honored every individual's basic humanity. It stuck with me.

The sturdy heartwood holds it all together. As I drive home along rural highway 221, enjoying the rolling green farmland of the Willamette Valley, I notice an older woman driving the speed limit, closely followed by a sports car clinging two feet from her bumper. Many decide to move here for the idyllic peaceful landscape, but often seem to only recreate the values they left behind, unaware of the harm they are doing to long established local social mores.

During the horrible fire that plagued our summer in 2020, included in this book, my mother was called by a politician seeking feedback from the people in her district. My mom expressed concern from the evening our local news reported that a grandson, returning to save his grandmother from a burning home, had died in the effort. Oregonians were all solemn and sad that night, but the whiskey bar roared with drunken laughter.

"I wish we could somehow stop that," my mother said, "show a little more respect."

The politician went silent for a moment, "you know you are the eighth person who told me this tonight?"

Please understand that Oregon is more than just a retirement backdrop. Those of us who reside here enjoy the benefits of clean air, quiet beaches, and an original habitat that supports White Crowned Sparrows, Stellar Jays, Cooper's Hawks, Chickadees and a variety of additional wildlife. To us, they are part of our communities. When some new arrivals use their affluence, without consideration of the values they are changing, it tends to demean a community that doesn't consider their status as coming before local livability. While I can appreciate your home theater, Mercedes sports car, new speed boat, and other items, they are not necessarily the things I, nor others, wish to define ourselves by. Please honor the Oregonian culture we are so proud of.

"Heaven is under our feet
as well as over our heads."

-Henry David Thoreau